Standards and Guidelines for

Adult Day Services

Young America, Minnesota 55397-0134

Prepared by
Mary Brugger Murphy
and
The National Adult Day Services Association
a unit of
The National Council on the Aging, Inc.

As adopted by
The NADSA Delegate Council and
The NCOA Board of Directors

March 1997

Made possible by grants from

Active Services Corporation
Bell Atlantic in conjunction with the CWA and IBEW Unions
Grotta Foundation for Senior Care
Metropolitan Life Foundation
Ross Products Division, Abbott Laboratories
U S WEST in conjunction with the CWA and IBEW Unions

Published by The National Council on the Aging, Inc.
409 Third Street SW, Suite 200
Washington, DC 20024

Standards and Guidelines for Adult Day Services is a new, revised edition of *Standards and Guidelines for Adult Day Care*, 1990, which was a revised edition of the *Standards for Adult Day Care*, originally published in 1984. Third Edition, Copyright©1997
Printed in the United States of America. 1997, 2K

Library of Congress Cataloging-in-Publication Data

National Adult Day Services Association (U.S.)
        Standards and guidelines for adult day services / prepared by Mary Brugger Murphy and the National Adult Day Services Association, a unit of The National Council on the Aging, Inc.; as adopted by the NASDA Delegate Council and the NCOA Board of Directors. --3rd ed.

        p.   cm

        Rev. ed of: Standards and guidelines for adult day care / prepared by the National Institute on Adult Daycare. 2nd ed. 1990.

        "March 1997."
        Includes index.
        ISBN 0-910883-86-6
        1. Day care centers for the aged--Standards--United States.
I. Murphy, Mary Brugger. II. The National Council on the Aging. III. National Adult Day Services Association (U.S.) Standards and guidelines for adult day care. IV. Title.

HV1461.N364   1997
362.6'3--dc21   97-31313
                                                                                                          CIP

CONTENTS

Adult Day Services: A Definition

Adult day services are community-based group programs designed to meet the needs of adults with impairments through individual plans of care. These structured, comprehensive, nonresidential programs provide a variety of health, social, and related support services in a protective setting. By supporting families and other caregivers, adult day services enable participants to live in the community.

Adult day services assess the needs of participants and offer services to meet those needs. Participants attend on a planned basis.

Statement of Rights and Responsibilities of Adult Day Services Participants

The following is a statement of rights of persons enrolled in adult day services programs. Though the statement is not intended to be inclusive, it suggests an outline of the basic rights that should be guaranteed to adult day services participants.

- The right to be treated as an adult, with consideration, respect, and dignity, including privacy in treatment and in care for personal needs;

- The right to participate in a program of services and activities designed to encourage independence, learning, growth, and awareness of constructive ways to develop one's interests and talents;

- The right to self-determination within the day services setting, including the opportunity to:
  - participate in developing or changing one's plan for services;
  - decide whether or not to participate in any given activity;
  - be involved to the extent possible in program planning and operation;
  - refuse treatment and be informed of the consequences of such refusal;
  - end participation in the adult day center at any time;

- The right to a thorough initial assessment, development of an individualized plan of care, and a determination of the required level of care;

- The right to be cared for in an atmosphere of sincere interest and concern in which needed support and services are provided;

- The right to a safe, secure, and clean environment;

- The right to receive nourishment and assistance with meals as necessary to maximize functional abilities and quality of life;

- The right to confidentiality and the guarantee that no personal or medical information will be released to persons not authorized under law to receive it without the participant's written consent;

- The right to voice grievances about care or treatment without discrimination or reprisal;

- The right to be fully informed, as documented by the participant's written acknowledgment, of all participant's rights and responsibilities and of all rules and regulations regarding participant conduct and responsibilities;

- The right to be free from harm, including unnecessary physical or chemical restraint, isolation, excessive medication, abuse, or neglect;

- The right to be fully informed, at the time of acceptance into the program, of services and activities available and related charges;

- The right to communicate with others and be understood by them to the extent of the participant's capability.

Participants also have responsibilities. To the extent possible, the responsibilities are to be carried out by the participant—or by the caregiver on behalf of the participant, if necessary. These responsibilities include:

- The responsibility to treat personnel with respect and courtesy;

- The responsibility to communicate with staff to develop a relationship of trust;

- The responsibility to make appropriate choices and seek appropriate care;

- The responsibility to ask questions and confirm understanding of instructions;

- The responsibility to share opinions, concerns, and complaints with the director.

Preface

Pat Shull, Chair, National Adult Day Services Association

In 1993 the Delegate Council of the National Institute on Adult Daycare identified as a major concern the lack of definition and structure in the adult day services field. The Delegate Council recognized that while adult day centers need flexibility to meet the needs of the communities they serve, they should have a consistent set of guidelines to follow. These guidelines also clarify for funders what they are purchasing. It was determined that adult day centers might best be defined in terms of levels of care provided. Once the levels of care were defined, then the *Standards and Guidelines* would need to be revised to incorporate those definitions and the principles they reflected.

During the process of defining the levels, and then revising the standards, we sought and received input from the field. The high volume of response reflected the high level of interest. The Standards Task Force took the responses very seriously, considering each one point by point. The input from the field influenced many aspects of the standards, and prompted many changes in the final version of the standards.

Two additional changes in approach make these standards quite different from the 1990 edition—and both of these changes reflect the growth in our field. First, the standards are less "educational" in content and in tone than they were in 1990. In 1990 the standards were "all we had." Now we have additional educational pieces, with even more in process. Second, the standards have been pared down to simpler, more universal statements of what should be. This format is appropriate for standards that will help formulate criteria for accreditation.

These standards will help us to continue clarifying and strengthening our role in improving the lives of our participants.

Foreword

Becky Groff, Chair, Task Force on the Revision of the Standards and Guidelines

"If you want to teach people a new way of thinking, don't bother trying to teach them. Instead, give them a tool...." Buckminster Fuller, futurist.

Adult day services have reached a new frontier, challenging us to find new, different ways to meet the needs of the people we serve and their families. The 1997 revision of the *Standards and Guidelines for Adult Day Services* is a tool intended to define the current scope of practice in the field of adult day services. The field of adult day services is experiencing tremendous growth. While we embrace growth, it challenges us with many changes. We have worked to encompass in this tool the diversity and scope of those changes.

A wide range of constituents participated in the revision process. Funders, regulators, clinicians, providers, advocates, and staff worked countless hours to craft a document that would define the scope of practice in adult day services. The input from the committee, the Delegate Council, and the field gave invaluable direction in refining the standards.

This standards document lays out core, enhanced, and intensive levels of service. Providers, after themselves defining the level of services they will provide, have a mechanism to design their programs in response to their own unique community needs. The document is not intended to be instructional or prescriptive, but to set forth these essential aspects of a sound program at several levels. It is intended to be a guide in the development and administration of a quality program and quality services.

We are grateful for the generous support of all of the funders who made this endeavor possible: Active Services Corporation, Bell Atlantic, Grotta Foundation for Senior Care, Metropolitan Life Foundation, Ross Products Division of Abbott Laboratories, and U S WEST.

National Adult Day Services Association (NADSA) Delegate Council, 1997-1998

CHAIR
Pat Shull
Executive Director
Adult Care of Chester County
Exton, Pennsylvania

CHAIR-ELECT
Jan Nestler
Executive Director
Eastside Adult Day Center
Bellevue, Wisconsin

SECRETARY
Judith Kratzner
Director
Indiana Association of Area Agencies
  on Aging
Anderson, Indiana

TREASURER
Elgie E. (Bubba) Justice, Jr.
Active Services Corporation
Birmingham, Alabama

PAST CHAIR
Paulette Z. Geller
Executive Director, Older Adult Services
Winter Park Health Foundation
Miller Center for Older Adults
Winter Park, Florida

AT-LARGE DELEGATES
Linda Adams Martin
Director, Community Programs
Foundation for Senior Living
Phoenix, Arizona

Nancy J. Cox
Deputy Director
Partners in Caregiving
Bowman Gray School of Medicine
Winston-Salem, North Carolina

Jed D. Johnson
Executive Director
Home and Community Services
Jewish Association on Aging
Pittsburgh, Pennsylvania

Kathy Hoernig
Administrator of Geriatric Services
Medical University of South Carolina
Charleston, South Carolina

Rosa Ramirez
Project Director
Alzheimer's Association
Los Angeles, California

Jim Soos
Project Manager
Brookdale National Group Respite Program
Berkeley, California

REGIONAL DELEGATES

REGION I (CT, ME, MA, NH, RI, VT)
Elaine T. Fluet
Chief Operating Officer
Gardner Visiting Nurse Association
Gardner, Massachusetts

REGION II (NY, NJ, PR)
Brenda Sobeck
Program Director
St. James Mercy Hospital
Hornell, New York

REGION III (DE, DC, MD, PA, VA, WV)
Karen Leachman
Executive Director
Wood County Senior Citizens Assoc., Inc.
Parkersburg, West Virginia

REGION IV (AL, FL, GA, KY, MS, NC, SC, TN)
Jean Reaves
Executive Director
Roanoke Valley Adult Day Center, Inc.
Weldon, North Carolina

REGION V (IL, IN, MI, MN, OH, WI)
Diana Brown
Manager, Adult Services Division
Curative Rehabilitation Center
Green Bay, Wisconsin

REGION VI (AR, LA, NM, OK, TX)
Loretta Echols
Director of Purchased Services
East Arkansas Area Agency on Aging
Jonesboro, Arkansas

REGION VII (IA, KS, MO, NE)
Becky Groff
Director
Wesley Methodist Adult Day Center
Des Moines, Iowa

REGION VIII (CO, MT, ND, SD, UT, WY)
Bonnie Baird Smith
Director
Sunshine Terrace Adult Day Center
Logan, Utah

REGION IX (AZ, CA, HI, NV)
Nancy Brundy
Director of Aging Health Services
Goldman Institute on Aging
San Francisco, California

REGION X (AK, ID, OR, WA)
Jesalyn Stanton
Adult Day Center Supervisor
Salvation Army Serendipity Adult Day Center
Anchorage, Alaska

NADSA Task Force on Standards 1996-1997

CHAIR

Becky Groff
Director
Wesley Methodist Adult Day Center
Des Moines, Iowa

MEMBERS

Dr. C. Jean Blaser
Manager
Illinois Department on Aging
Long Term Care Division
Springfield, Illinois

Judy Canterbury, RN, GNP, MSN
Executive Director
Western Institute Foundation for
   Mental Health
Oceanside, California

Belinda Eichler
Product Director
Prudential
Roseland, New Jersey

Sandra Fresh, RN
VA Medical Center
Portland, Oregon

Charlette Gallagher-Allred, Ph.D., RD
Manager, Geriatrics & LTC Services
Ross Products Division
Abbott Laboratories
Columbus, Ohio

Paulette Z. Geller
Executive Director, Older Adult Services
Winter Park Health Foundation
Miller Center for Older Adults
Winter Park, Florida

Sandra Harmon-Weiss, MD
Head of Government Programs
AETNA US Healthcare
Blue Bell, Pennsylvania

Kathy Hoernig, NHA
Administrator of Geriatric Services
Medical University of South Carolina
Charleston, South Carolina

Eileen Lynette
Elder Care Practice Leader
Kaiser Permanente Consulting
Kaiser Foundation Hospitals
Oakland, California

Clare Scott
Senior Project Manager
The Partnership Group
Blue Bell, Pennsylvania

Patricia A. Shull
Executive Director
Adult Care of Chester County
Exton, Pennsylvania

Bonnie Baird Smith
Director
Sunshine Terrace Adult Day Center
Logan, Utah

CONTRIBUTORS

Art Godin*
AETNA US Healthcare
Blue Bell, Pennsylvania

Jan Hickey
Adult Day Care Specialist
Illinois Department on Aging
Long Term Care Division
Springfield, Illinois

Kara Kennedy
Patient and Family Services
Alzheimer's Association
Chicago, Illinois

Mary Tellis-Nayak, RN, MSN, MPH*
Long Term Care Accreditation Services
JCAHO
Oakbrook, Illinois

Ann Marie Watson
The Partnership Group
Blue Bell, Pennsylvania

*Formerly associated with

STAFF

Mary Brugger Murphy, MLA
Director
National Adult Day Services Association
Washington, DC

INTRODUCTION

REVISION OF STANDARDS

The Standards Task Force that met to revise the *1990 Standards and Guidelines for Adult Day Care* began by approving answers to key questions about the *Standards:*

What is a standard?

- a means to define parameters of practice;
- a rule, principle, or measure established by authority;
- a model or example;
- a criterion or test of quality.

What are the strengths of the 1990 *Standards*?

- the focus on quality and corresponding philosophy of quality enhancement;
- provision of a structure for programs;
- guidance on implementation;
- explanation of the intent behind the standards;
- flexibility;
- readability;
- user-friendliness;
- inclusivity.

Why revise the *Standards*?

- to expand upon the 1990 *Standards* and further increase service quality;
- to update the terminology;
- to identify distinctions among the ranges or levels of care;
- to acknowledge increasing diversity in adult day service programs;
- to further promote consumer-centered day services;
- to prepare for embarking upon program accreditation.

Who are the stakeholders in the *Standards*?

The stakeholders are the consumers (participants and family/caregivers) and the providers (both existing and potential), including nursing homes, assisted living facilities, home health agencies, hospitals, and senior centers, as well as those operating free-standing centers. Funders, regulators, referral sources, payers, and legislators are also stakeholders.

What is the purpose of the revision?

The purpose is to enhance the role of adult day services in the constellation of care and to develop participant-focused standards for providers, regulators, and payers.

Further, the purpose is:
- to insure consumer/payer protection;
- to provide measurable accountability for regulators;
- to educate providers;
- to move toward a seal of approval;
- to lay the groundwork for program accreditation;
- to promote the growth of quality centers;
- to direct centers toward an increase in participant-focus;
- to recognize the diversity of needs of both programs and clients;
- to recognize overall changes in the health care system; and
- to boost quality assurance.

RANGES AND LEVELS OF CARE

The concept of levels of care has been adopted in response to the significant changes in the field of adult day services during the last ten years and in preparation for changes anticipated in the near future. These changes include, for example, the increase in the number of programs and participants, the increase in acuity level and health care needs of participants, and the decrease in functional level and independence among those served. The adult day services programs that serve such individuals have already adapted their programs to respond to these changes. As centers have adapted, so must NADSA modify its definitions, labels, and expectations to ensure the accuracy and appropriateness of its designations. NADSA strongly feels that, in view of the field's increasing maturity, levels of care should be delineated and reflected in the national standards for adult day service programs.

As always in adult day services, the starting point is the individual participant, whose needs form the core of this vision. The care must then revolve around participant needs and employ services that allow the participant to function at the highest level of his or her ability.

When NADSA circulated the draft standards for comments from the field, it became clear that designating "Levels of Need 1, 2, and 3" and "Levels or Ranges of Care 1, 2, and 3" was unacceptable to many NADSA members because needs of participants could not be so simplistically delineated and assigning numbers to these levels implied different values, rather than categories.

Therefore, the standards do not define levels of need; rather they emphasize the importance of individual assessments and individualized plans of care. Three types of services are distinguished—according to staff time and training and intensity of services. These service categories are core services, enhanced services, and intensive services.

The actual provisions of the ranges or levels of care are an integral part of the standards themselves.

However, a brief overview may be helpful: The three ranges or levels of care all start with the following core services: assessment and care planning, assistance with ADLs, health-related services, social services, therapeutic activities, nutrition, transportation, and emergency care. The most important distinction between these services and the core services delineated in the 1990 *Standards* is the change from nursing services in the *Standards* to "health-related services" here. At the core services level, no nursing services are required, and no nurse is required. The participant who needs nursing services needs enhanced or intensive services.

Core services, in very brief summary, include the core services listed above but do not provide direct nursing, rehabilitative, or psychosocial services.

Enhanced services may add to the core services some or all of the following: restorative, supportive, or rehabilitative nursing care on a moderate basis (that is, intermittent but not continuous); assessment and referral for psychosocial services and follow-through with recommended treatments in the plan of care; and physical, occupational, and speech therapy at a functional maintenance level.

Intensive services may add some or all of these services: intensive nursing services necessary for unstable medical conditions; therapies at a restorative or rehabilitative level; intensive psychosocial services; and specialized supportive services, as needed.

WHEN CORE, ENHANCED, OR INTENSIVE SERVICES ARE NEEDED

Core services:
The participant who receives core services needs socialization, some supervision, supportive service, and minimal assistance with ADLs. This person may have multiple physical problems but is stable and does not need nursing observation or nursing intervention. There may be some cognitive impairment, but the resulting behavior can be handled with redirection and reassurance. This participant can communicate (though not necessarily verbalize) personal needs.

Enhanced services:
The participant who receives enhanced services needs moderate assistance. He or she may need health assessment, oversight, or monitoring by a nurse; therapy services at a functional maintenance level; or moderate assistance with 1-3 ADLs. He or she may have difficulty communicating or making appropriate judgments or may periodically demonstrate disruptive behavior that can be accommodated—with increased skills or time on the part of the staff.

Intensive services:

The participant who receives intensive services needs maximum assistance. His or her medical condition may not be stable and may require regular monitoring or intervention by a nurse. Rehabilitative or restorative therapy services may be needed. There may be a need for total care in one or more ADLs, or moderate assistance with more than three ADLs at the center, or a need for a two-person assist. The individual may be unable to communicate needs or may display behavior requiring frequent staff intervention or support—and even more skills or time on the part of the staff.

IMPORTANCE OF ASSESSMENT AND INDIVIDUALIZED PLAN OF CARE

In order for any individual to be served appropriately in adult day services, a thorough initial assessment is essential. If the basic assessment indicates a need for further evaluation in a specific area, then additional resources need to be available for a more extensive assessment. As a result of the initial assessment, a plan of care is developed to describe the range or level of care needed. Ongoing assessments will assure continued placement in the appropriate level and continued provision of appropriate services. However, change in a single indicator may not necessarily cause movement from one level or range to another.

MEETING CHANGING NEEDS OF PARTICIPANTS

An adult day services program can serve individuals needing different levels or ranges of care at any one time, so that most individuals' changing needs can be met within the center. The center that provides only core services may need to make some adjustments in order to respond to changing needs. If a participant served in a center providing only core services needs short-term care beyond the scope provided, then the center is responsible for arranging for that care. This may mean making arrangements for additional services on a consultative basis, or making a referral for additional services, or it may mean that the individual can now only come to the center when specialized staff is available. The center is responsible for responding to changes in participant needs.

Furthermore, an individual to be served with core services must have stable health; and a required pre-admission assessment by a health care professional must include assurance of that stability. Periodic reassessments will ensure the continued appropriateness of the placement or indicate a need for change. Also essential is a pre-admission agreement signed by the participant and/or family/caregiver that clearly states under what circumstances the participant can continue to be served by that program.

HOW RADICAL A CHANGE?

The 1990 *Standards* clearly state that a center must assess the needs of participants and identify the necessary, corresponding services as it defines its target population and establishes its care and service package. Those standards admonish centers to be prepared to respond to real needs and not to attempt to serve individuals whose needs are outside the scope and intensity of service planned. The articulation of the levels or ranges of core, enhanced, and intensive services simply help the center to draw the lines. They are intended to clarify categories and provide a framework for making decisions on the target population and components of care.

SERVING PARTICIPANTS WITH COGNITIVE IMPAIRMENTS

The majority of adult day service programs serve individuals with cognitive impairment. The standards clarify how, as the needs of those individuals change and require more staff time and skills, the enhanced and intensive services levels will offer appropriately increased services, staff time, and training. In the definitions of levels, the time and skills required to respond to challenging behaviors are given the same consideration and same weight as the time and skills required to respond to physical needs.

Adult day services strive to provide the exact services the individual needs. When a program serves individuals whose functional levels and behaviors require intensive staff interaction, the program should provide the needed intensive staff interaction—but not necessarily physical, occupational, or speech therapy. Such therapy is provided to the individual who needs and will benefit from that service.

Two factors in adult day programs take on added importance when serving participants with cognitive impairments:(1) the role of the family and/or caregiver, and (2) the use of adult day services to offer respite.

(1) In these programs, the family or caregiver, as well as the participant, is a client of the center. These guidelines address the many points at which the family/caregiver must be involved. Family members other than the primary caregiver may also need to be involved in service and placement decisions and processes.

(2) Respite, or relief, is one of the benefits of adult day services. The program not only provides essential relief to the family/caregiver, but it also offers respite to the participant —that is, a change from the home environment and from the expectations and emotions of the family/caregiver—and an opportunity to interact with others.

Note: This text contains some references to serving individuals with cognitive impairments, but there are no separate sections on serving any individuals with specific diagnoses. The Standards Task Force found that most guidelines for serving those with dementia could and should be incorporated into the basic standards and guidelines, because many special considerations for participants with dementia actually applied to all participants.

BEYOND THE CORE

Programs and populations vary—and they change daily with changes in functional levels of participants. Adult day programs must be prepared to respond to a wide range of participant needs. Centers whose participants currently may not need extensive medical and therapeutic services may at some point in the future find that they need to provide or arrange for additional services.

These standards are intended to describe a foundation of quality care appropriate for all types of adult day programs—and to offer a blueprint for the future for programs providing core services.

FLEXIBILITY

The 1990 *Standards* presented an official statement on flexibility, which NADSA considers a key element in the success of adult day services programs. Flexibility is important to protect evolving programs, encourage innovation, and lead to the acceptance of modifications that permit programs to grow while continuing to provide appropriate care to participants. NADSA offers the following statement on flexibility:

NADSA recognizes the variety and richness of adult day programs. Developing standards that are appropriate for all programs is difficult. It is not possible to foresee all the various circumstances that may occur. Therefore, NADSA recommends that state licensing, certifying, funding, accrediting, and/or monitoring agencies incorporate into their laws, regulations, policies, and guidelines the authority to grant program flexibility, that is, the approval of alternative ways to meet the intent of a standard so long as safe and quality care is provided.

FEDERAL, STATE, AND LOCAL REQUIREMENTS

It is essential for readers to understand that federal, state, and local laws, ordinances, regulations, and requirements always take precedence over these recommended, voluntary standards.

FORMAT

The following format is used for the statements that follow. The actual standards are numbered and include the word "shall." Sometimes the standard is followed by a statement of intent in order to clarify the reason for including the standard. Often the standard is followed by guidelines, in order to provide more detail or direction in carrying out the standard. The guidelines are not part of the standard. Compliance with the standard does not depend upon compliance with the guidelines.

For example,

187	Applicants, participants and ......

Intent:
In order to....

Guidelines:
This includes the following:...

Further, if there are differences in the standards or guidelines for the three levels or ranges of care, then they are identified as appropriate for *Core*, *Enhanced*, or *Intensive Services*.

PART ONE: TARGET POPULATION

BACKGROUND

Adult day services are evolving programs, responding to changing needs of communities and individual participants. The target population(s) will vary within and among settings and will reflect community needs; licensing and funding requirements; the center's assessment of participants' needs; resources such as space and staff; and the parent organization's philosophy and mission.

The population served will vary according to the identified needs of the community and the goals, resources, and capability of the organization providing the service. The target population includes one or more of the following groups of individuals.

Adults with physical, psychosocial, or mental impairments who require assistance and supervision, such as:

- persons who have few or inadequate support systems;
- persons who require assistance with activities of daily living (ADLs) and instrumental activities of daily living (IADLs);
- persons with physical problems that require health or medical monitoring and regular supervision;
- persons with emotional problems that interfere with their ability to cope on a daily basis;
- persons with memory loss and cognitive impairment that interfere with daily functioning;
- persons with developmental disabilities;
- persons who need nutritional intervention;
- persons who require assistance in overcoming the isolation associated with functional limitations or disabilities; and
- persons whose families and/or caregivers need respite.

Adults who need rehabilitative therapy (including restorative therapy and functional maintenance therapy) in order to restore or maintain an optimum level of functioning, such as:

- persons recently discharged from hospitals or nursing homes;
- persons needing therapy because of some chronic disability, to adjust to their limitations and learn adaptive skills;
- persons who, without program intervention, are at risk of premature institutionalization because of physical deterioration or their psychological condition;

- persons who need support in making the transition from independent living to group care or in making the transition from group care to independent living.

Adults who require services provided by or under the supervision of an appropriately licensed nurse or other licensed health care professional in accordance with federal and state requirements. Such services include:

- assessment;
- supervision or administration of medications and observation of their effects;
- treatments, including medical nutrition therapy;
- health education and training in self care, including training in self-medication;
- training in activities of daily living (ADLs);
- assistance in ADLs;
- medical monitoring; and
- medical therapies or treatments.

1	Each adult day center shall define the target population(s) it intends to serve.

Guideline:

The center will consider the needs of the participants and the availability, frequency, scope, and intensity of services necessary to meet those needs. Each center will determine the levels of need of the individuals it plans to serve and evaluate its capacity to provide the corresponding level or range of care.

2	Each adult day center shall serve only participants whose needs while at the center do not exceed the center's resources and not serve those who would be served more appropriately in a different setting.

Guideline:

A guiding principle for all adult day centers is neither to knowingly admit nor to continue caring for participants whose needs cannot be met by the program directly or in cooperation with outside resources.

<table>
<tr><td>

3

</td><td>

Each center shall have a mission and philosophy statement that reflects the needs of the participants and the care and services it is committed to providing.

</td></tr>
</table>

Guideline:

Target populations may change, depending on need, and services will need to change. Services offered must meet the needs of participants. The configuration of a particular center at a given time reflects these influences.

DETERMINING AN APPROPRIATE TARGET POPULATION

<table>
<tr><td>

4

</td><td>

Each adult day center shall have a written policy on participants who are appropriate and those who may not be appropriate for enrollment.

</td></tr>
</table>

Guidelines:

A written statement that reflects that policy should be part of the intake agreement with the participant and family/caregiver at the time of enrollment and should be agreed to and signed by the participant, if possible, and/or the family/caregiver. (See "Part Three: Individualized Plan of Care," Intake Screening, page 33)

The appropriate target population(s) will vary within and among settings, depending on community needs, staffing, and service availability. Generally, those who may not be appropriate for enrollment include adults whose need for care requires staff time and skills different from those the individual program is able and qualified to provide, as well as adults who are best served in a less structured setting.

Participants who are inappropriate for all adult day service programs include:

- Adults who are bedfast or do not have the strength or the stamina to attend adult day services for the minimum required hours as defined in state licensing requirements.

- Adults in an infectious stage of a communicable disease, unless a physician states there is no significant hazard. (They should only be admitted under guidance of the health department and/or licensing authority.) This policy is intended to protect the health of the center participants and is not intended to discriminate against any individual.

- Adults with emotional or behavioral disorders who are destructive to self or others or disruptive in a group setting—unless the center has the capacity, including qualified staff, to adequately and appropriately manage these problems.

- Adults who are too independent to benefit from the activities and services provided in the adult day center, and who need referral to other more appropriate and available programs such as a senior center or nutrition site.

5	Each center shall conduct an assessment of each potential participant in order to determine whether or not that participant is included in the center's target population and whether or not the center can meet the participant's needs.

6	Center policies shall define the target population, admission criteria, discharge criteria, medication policy, participant rights, confidentiality, and grievance procedures.

PART TWO: ADMINISTRATION AND ORGANIZATION

THE GOVERNING BODY

7 Each adult day services center shall have a governing body with full legal authority and fiduciary responsibility for the overall operation of the program in accordance with applicable state and federal requirements.

Guidelines:
Responsibilities of the governing body include:
- defining the governing body's composition and size;
- determining the center's program and operating policies;
- developing an organizational structure that defines lines of authority to implement the program and policies;
- appointing and evaluating and/or approving the appointment of a qualified administrator;
- determining the scope and quality of services provided to participants and families/caregivers in response to defined need (See "Part One: Target Population," page 17);
- establishing an advisory committee;
- reviewing and overseeing the center's fiscal affairs, including adopting an annual budget, setting fees, and managing financial risk;
- arranging for any necessary program and/or financial audits or reviews;
- developing short- and long-range plans;
- conducting periodic programmatic and key staff evaluations;
- ensuring the program's continual compliance with and conformity to all relevant federal, state, local, or municipal laws and/or regulations that govern operation of adult day service facilities;
- approving or authorizing written agreements and collaborative relations with other agencies for specified services;
- approving and participating in plans for acquisition of funds (such as fund-raising events, capital campaigns, grants, and contributions for not-for-profits and selling of shares, raising venture capital, and loans for for-profits);
- approving and participating in plans for public relations and marketing;
- risk management; and
- oversight of the quality improvement plan.

21

THE ADVISORY COMMITTEE

8 Each adult day services center shall have a body that serves as an advisory committee.

Guidelines:

For a single purpose agency, the governing body may fulfill the functions of the advisory committee if it meets the representation standard (See Standard 10, page 23), or a separate advisory committee may be established.

When an adult day center is a subdivision or subunit of a multifunctional organization, a committee or subcommittee of the governing body of the multifunctional organization may serve as the advisory committee of the center.

Where there is a separate advisory committee, it is recommended that the chair of that committee serve as a voting member of the governing body.

The advisory committee meets regularly in order to review and make recommendations on program policies.

Those policies may include:
- scope and quality of services and activities provided;
- admission and discharge criteria;
- policies and practices for service records;
- quality assurance activities and findings and plan of corrective action;
- program evaluation; and
- fees.

9 The advisory committee shall be representative of the community and participant population.

Guideline:

The advisory committee should include family members of current or past participants and non-voting staff representatives. The advisory committee should include professionals and/or consumer representatives with knowledge of the population served, including representatives of participants with special needs, with cognitive impairments, or of diverse cultures.

A WRITTEN PLAN OF OPERATION

10 The governing body shall review, approve, and revise a current, written plan of operation.

Guidelines:
The plan should include, but is not limited to:
- a mission statement;
- short- and long-range program goals;
- outcome measures;
- definition of the target population, including number, age, and needs of participants;
- geographical definition of the service area;
- hours and days of operation;
- description of basic services and any optional services;
- policies and procedures for service delivery;
- policies and procedures for admission and discharge;
- policies and procedures for assessment and reassessment and for a plan of care developed by an interdisciplinary team with the input of participants and/or family/caregiver;
- staffing pattern;
- a plan for utilizing community resources;
- facility planning and maintenance;
- policies and procedures for recruitment, orientation, training, evaluation, and professional development of staff;
- policies and procedures for recruiting, orientation, training, and evaluation of volunteers;
- general record policies;
- statement of participant rights and family/caregiver rights;
- mandated reporting procedures;
- marketing plan;
- strategic plan;
- accident, illness, and emergency procedures;
- grievance procedures;
- procedures for reporting suspected abuse;
- operational budget; and
- quality improvement plan.

A WRITTEN EMERGENCY PLAN

11 A written plan for handling emergencies shall be developed and be easily accessible in the center and in all center vehicles.

Guidelines:
Centers should also have:
- staff training to ensure smooth implementation of the emergency plan;
- equipment available to support implementation of the emergency plan; and
- sufficient staff trained in CPR and first aid to assure that at least two staff members (one of whom is trained in CPR) are in the center at all times during hours of operation when more than one participant is present. Two staff members are required so that one can attend to the emergency and the second attend to the other participant(s) in the center.

12 Plans for evacuation and relocation of participants shall be in place in the event of a power outage or other emergency situation.

Guideline:
Detailed plans should be negotiated early, with as many options as possible. Licensing requirements for the day center and the alternate emergency facility must be comparable.

LINES OF SUPERVISION AND RESPONSIBILITY

13 An organizational chart shall be developed to illustrate the lines of authority and communication channels, and shall be provided to all staff.

Guideline:
To ensure continuity of direction and supervision, responsibilities should be clearly divided between the governing body and the adult day services administrator.

14

The administrator shall have full authority and responsibility to plan, staff, direct, implement, and evaluate the program.

Guideline:

The administrator also has responsibility for establishing collaborative relationships with other community organizations to ensure that necessary support services are available to participants and their families/caregivers.

15

The administrator or the individual(s) designated by the administrator shall be on site to provide the center's day-to-day management during hours of operation.

Guideline:

If the administrator is responsible for more than one site, or has duties not related to adult day services administration or provision of services, a program director should be designated for each additional site, should be on site, and should report to the administrator (See " Part Five: Staffing," page 70).

ADMINISTRATIVE POLICIES AND PROCEDURES

FISCAL SYSTEM

16

Each adult day center shall demonstrate fiscal responsibility and accountability.

17	Fiscal policies, procedures, and records shall be developed to enable the administrator to meet fiscal reporting needs of the governing body and funders.

Guidelines:

The fiscal system should:
- use generally accepted principles of accounting;
- identify all direct and indirect costs incurred by the adult day services center;
- provide for a planning process to develop annual and projected day services center budgets, including specific cost allocations, year-end reconciliation, and cost reporting;
- provide documentation needed for financial audits, including in-kind contributions;
- provide periodic financial statements containing a balance sheet, statement of revenue and expenses, and changes in financial condition;
- allow monitoring of expenditures by identifying budget variances;
- project cash flow and sources of revenue;
- provide records of expenditures with supporting documentation;
- maintain billing and collection records;
- provide for annual audit;
- ensure payment of payroll taxes;
- provide for timely submission of fiscal reports required by funding source(s);
- track in-kind contributions; and
- provide for participant financial records, including service and attendance reports.

FINANCIAL PLAN

18	Each adult day center shall develop a plan to address the long-term financial needs of the program.

Guidelines:

The plan should include projected program growth, capital purchases, projected revenue, projected expenses, and plans for acquisition of funds needed, either through venture capital or fund-raising.

19

A fee schedule shall be formally established and should include any eligibility for discounts, waivers, or deferral of payment.

QUALITY IMPROVEMENT PLAN

20

Each adult day center shall develop a written continuous quality improvement plan that is updated annually.

Intent:
Quality improvement activities are designed to promote continuous quality improvement and safeguard or improve care by assessing the value of care or a service and taking action to improve that quality.

Guideline:
The continuous quality improvement plan should have specific measurable objectives, meet requirements of licensing and funding sources, and meet professional standards of practice with outcome measures to determine the efficacy of adult day services.

PERSONNEL POLICIES AND PRACTICES

21

The organization shall provide an adequate number of staff whose qualifications are commensurate with defined job responsibilities and applicable licensure, law and regulation, and/or certification.

22

Processes shall be designed to ensure that the competence of all staff members is regularly assessed, maintained, demonstrated, and improved.

23

All employees and volunteers shall be provided orientation and in-service training.

(See "Training" in "Part Five: Staffing," page 68)

PARTICIPANT POLICIES

24

Adult day services shall be culturally and linguistically responsive and respectful. No individual shall be excluded from participation in or be denied the benefits of or be otherwise subjected to discrimination in the adult day services program on the grounds of race, sex, religion, national origin, sexual orientation, or disability.

25

Adult day services shall promote a restraint-free environment. The use of chemical and/or physical restraints shall be restricted to those whose physicians have ordered such restraints and shall meet provisions for their use as determined by accepted standards of practice. (See the requirements of the Omnibus Budget Reconciliation Act, 1987.)

26

A participant bill of rights and responsibilities shall be developed, posted, distributed, and explained to all participants or their representatives, families, staff, and volunteers in the language understood by the individual.

27

A grievance procedure shall be established to enable participants and their families/caregivers to have their concerns addressed without fear of recrimination.

28

All centers, including those not covered by the Patient Self-Determination Act, shall maintain written policies and procedures on how the Patient Self-Determination Act will be implemented in the program.

Guidelines:

Centers will:
- make advance directive forms available to participants and their families/caregivers;
- provide resources to aid the participant in completing advance directives;
- advise the participant if the adult day program's policy and procedure for handling emergencies is or is not compatible with his or her expressed wishes to withhold emergency measures.

29

The center shall comply with the state mandatory or voluntary procedure for reporting suspected adult abuse to the adult protective service agency. Staff shall be trained in signs and indicators of potential abuse.

Guideline:

Center policy should include a provision that staff must observe participants for signs of potential abuse, including verbal abuse, physical abuse, sexual abuse, emotional or psychological abuse, neglect, and financial or material exploitation.

30

The center shall have a non-discrimination policy that recognizes and respects racial, ethnic, and cultural diversity.

Guidelines:

The non-discrimination policy and procedures developed are reflected in the center's:
- mission statement;
- governance and administration, including staffing;
- services and programs; and
- marketing and outreach.

GENERAL RECORD POLICIES

> **31**   Each adult day center shall maintain a participant record system.

Guidelines:

The participant record system should include, but is not limited to
- a permanent registry of all participants with dates of admission and discharge;
- a written policy on confidentiality and the protection of records that defines procedures governing their use and removal, and conditions for release of information contained in the records;
- a written policy on conditions that require authorization in writing by the participant or his/her legally responsible party for release of appropriate information not otherwise authorized by law;
- a written policy providing for the retention and storage of records for at least five (5) years (or in accordance with state or local requirements) from the date of the last service to the participant;
- a written policy, reflecting the requirements of funding sources and of state and local jurisdiction, on the retention and storage of such records in the event the center discontinues operation;
- a policy and procedure manual governing the record system and procedures for all agency staff; and
- maintenance of records in a secure storage area.

PARTICIPANT RECORDS

> **32**   The center shall maintain a record for each participant.

Guidelines:

This record should include, but is not limited to, the following:
- application and enrollment forms;
- medical history and functional assessment (initial and ongoing);
- nutritional status assessment;
- individual plan of care (initial and reviews) and revisions;
- fee determination sheet;
- service contract;
- signed authorizations for releases of medical information and photos, as appropriate;

- signed authorization for participant to receive emergency medical care if necessary;
- correspondence;
- attendance and service records;
- transportation plans;
- results of physical examination(s);
- where appropriate: medical information sheet; documentation of physicians' orders; treatment, therapy, medication, and professional notes;
- progress notes (chronological and timely);
- other notes and reports in the participant's record that are legibly recorded in a permanent material, dated, and signed by the recording person with his/her title;
- reviews of individual plans of care;
- discharge plan;
- current photograph of client;
- emergency contacts; and
- advance directive form or a statement that none has been signed.

ADMINISTRATIVE RECORDS

33   The center shall maintain administrative records.

Guidelines:
Administrative records include the following documents:
- personnel records (including personnel training);
- fiscal records;
- statistical records;
- government-related records (funding sources/regulatory);
- contracts;
- organizational records;
- results of utilization review and care plan audit;
- board meeting minutes;
- advisory committee minutes;
- certificates of annual fire and health inspections, and others as applicable;
- meals served, menu substitutions, therapeutic diets, nutritional supplements, food temperatures;
- incident reports;
- quality improvement minutes; and
- an historical record of policies and procedures.

COMMUNITY RELATIONS

34 The center staff and board shall have a system for informing the public about long-term care, adult day services, and about the center's programs and services.

INFORMATION AND REFERRAL

35 Applicants, participants and their families/caregivers shall be assisted in learning about the use of community agencies for financial, social, recreational, educational, and medical services.

Guideline:
Each center should maintain a community resource file.

SERVICE COORDINATION

36 The center staff shall establish linkages with other community agencies and institutions to coordinate services and form service networks.

PART THREE: INDIVIDUAL PLAN OF CARE

BACKGROUND

Each adult day center is responsible for completing an assessment and creating a service plan for each individual it intends to serve.

Each center will use the definitions and distinctions that it has chosen to describe its target population (See "Part One: Target Population," page 18.); it will plan to meet those participant needs by providing core, enhanced, and/or intensive services through the appropriate combination of time, skills, and resources by a staff trained to adapt to the needs of the target population.

The center may plan for the management of chronic and/or rehabilitative needs by providing appropriate services in a therapeutic milieu. The elements that make up this milieu include the environment, philosophy, and attitude of the staff as reflected in activities, services, and direct care. The goal of the program will be to strive for the greatest possible quality of life for each participant by maximizing the individual's potential strengths and skills.

ESSENTIAL PROGRAM COMPONENTS

37	Centers shall conduct an assessment and develop an individual written plan of care for each participant.

Guideline:
This plan of care must be based upon services needed and available. During this planning process the following eight steps will be completed in whatever order each adult day center considers appropriate.

STEP ONE — INTAKE SCREENING

38	The intake screening shall be completed in order to gain an initial sense of the appropriateness of the adult day services program for the individual.

Guidelines:
The screening, which is usually conducted in a telephone call with the individual, family, or referral source, or covered on an application form, should include:
- demographic information;
- referral source;
- consumer expectations;
- living arrangement;
- social history;
- financial status and insurance coverage;
- physical and mental health status, including diagnosis and current treatments
    (for example, the presence of feeding tubes or hydration lines);
- psychosocial status, including diagnosis, if any, and current treatments;
- name(s) of primary physician and other involved physicians;
- community agencies involved in providing services or support; and
- initial information on ADLs/IADLs.

If the client is determined at this point to be inappropriate, the center will not proceed with the remaining steps (See the chart that follows, page 40).

---

39   A medical report that reflects the current health status of the participant shall be obtained.

Intent:
The current health status of the participant must be included in the assessment.

---

40   Each participant shall designate a health provider to contact in the event of an emergency and for ongoing care.

STEP TWO—ENROLLMENT PROCESS

41 An enrollment agreement shall be completed and include:
- identification of services to be provided, agreed upon by the participant and/or caregiver and/or payer;
- a disclosure statement that describes the center's range of care and services;
- admission, discharge, and/or transfer criteria;
- fees and arrangements for reimbursement and payment; and
- identification of and authorization for third party payers.

42 The center shall have procedures for orientation of the participant and/or family/caregiver to policies, programs, and facilities.

43 The center shall assure that participants or their authorized representatives sign all consents and permission documents.

Guidelines:

These consents and permissions include:
- releases/requests for information;
- financing;
- emergencies;
- liability releases; and
- photo and trip releases.

44 The participant and family/caregiver shall be informed of the center's procedures for advance directives.

45 Each participant and caregiver shall receive written information regarding the criteria for transitions to a different level or range of services.

Intent:
For those centers that offer more than one level or range of services, the participant will be transitioned to a different level or range of services as his or her needs change.

STEP THREE — ASSESSMENT

 46 The center's assessment process shall identify the individual's strengths and needs, what services are required, and who is responsible for providing those services.

Intent:
A comprehensive written assessment is completed in order to collect sufficient information to develop the individual's plan of care. The assessment involves identifying the individual's strengths and needs and determining what services the individual requires from the center, either directly or through referral.

 47 The assessment shall be conducted by professional staff, paraprofessionals, consultants, or a combination thereof.

Guidelines:
A home visit by program staff or in coordination with community resources is advised during the admission assessment process. This visit helps identify home safety issues, home medication use, use of or need for adaptive equipment, and the in-home functioning of the participant and family/caregiver.

The assessment should include the person's physical and mental health profile (medical records, medical history, verification of medical regimen, nutritional status, primary physician and other specialists, and physician's restrictions), social history, formal and informal support systems, activities of daily living skills, mental and emotional status, community and financial resources, interests, hobbies, and past occupation. The assessment should also include

For potential participants with cognitive impairments, the assessment should address the following issues: personality, psychosocial background, diagnosis of cognitive impairments to rule out other possible causes of dementia, mental health status to rule out depression and other treatable conditions, level of interest in other people and things, mood, cognitive status/judgment, attention span, task focus, energy level, responsiveness to stimulation in the environment, distractibility, communication, sensory capacity, motor coordination, and spatial relationships. Special consideration should also be given to areas addressed for all participants, including ambulation, physical and functional capacity, physical and functional ADLs. If no diagnostic evaluation has been done, the participant and family/caregiver should be referred for evaluation.

STEP FOUR — WRITTEN INDIVIDUAL PLAN OF CARE

 48 A written plan of care shall be developed from the admission assessment for each participant.

Intent:
The plan of care and services and its implementation should be participant-oriented, flexible, and responsive to the participant's changing needs and abilities. The plan is intended to create a safe and supportive environment that promotes the participant's dignity and enhances the quality of life for the participant and the family/caregiver.

Guidelines:
Each individual's plan of care reflects the participant's abilities, strengths, and interests and includes:
  - identified needs in each service area;
  - time-limited measurable goal(s) and objectives of care for the participant (both long-term and short-term);
  - type and scope of interventions to be provided in order to reach desired, realistic outcomes;
  - discharge or transition plan, including specific criteria for discharge or transfer;
  - services to be provided by the center and by other sources to achieve the goal(s) and objectives; and
  - roles of participant, family/caregiver, support system and center staff and volunteers.

 49 The participant, caregiver, and other service providers shall have the opportunity to contribute to the development, implementation, and evaluation of the care plan.

STEP FIVE — CARE PLAN REVIEW AND REASSESSMENT

50 Reassessing the individual's needs and re-evaluating the appropriateness of service plans shall be done when needed—but at least semi-annually.

Intent:
Reassessment applies to the plan of care and ongoing comprehensive assessments as well as to the evaluation of goals and approaches that shape the plan of care.

Guideline:
Any significant change in the participant or family/caregiver status—such as hospitalization, changes in living arrangements, or modifications of the caregiver support system—will prompt the need for a reassessment and potential transition to a different range of care and services.

51 There shall be a care plan review with the participant and/or the family/caregiver that updates:
- scheduled days of attendance;
- services and goals of the plan of care; and
- conditions of participation.

STEP SIX — COORDINATION OF CARE

52 If coordination of care is needed and if the person is a client of another agency, then a care plan shall be developed in conjunction with the services provided by that agency.

Intent:
The extent of coordination of care for participants depends on the individual's specific needs and the degree to which the needs are met by the caregiver or another provider.

STEP SEVEN — SERVICE DOCUMENTATION

53 Progress notes shall be written and maintained as part of each participant's record.

Guideline:

Progress notes reflect timely reviews of the plan of care, changes in status, significant events, incidents, specific interventions and participant responses, and outside contacts such as telephone calls. Flow charts may be helpful in charting.

For the participant receiving core services, progress notes will be written to reflect changes in the individual's status, to record significant events/incidents, and to document at least a semi-annual review of the care plan.

STEP EIGHT — DISCHARGE PLAN

54 The center shall develop a discharge policy that includes criteria and notification procedures.

Guidelines:
Policy information includes:
- time frame for termination;
- criteria for discharge;
- notification procedures; and
- follow-up plan.

55 Discharge/transition plans shall be developed for those with changes in service need and changes in functional status that prompt another level of care.

Guidelines:
When appropriate for the participant, discharge procedures include:
- referrals to community service agencies for appropriate services;
- a discharge summary noting reasons for discharge and destination and including recommendations for continuing care; and
- follow-up when appropriate.

56 Each participant and family/caregiver shall receive notice if the participant is to be discharged from the program.

FLOW OF PROGRAM COMPONENTS

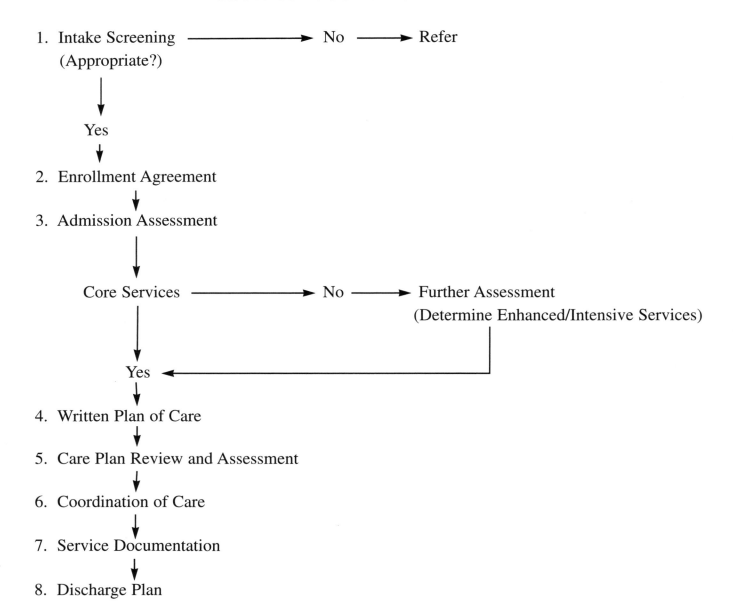

1. Intake Screening ————————→ No ——→ Refer
   (Appropriate?)

   ↓

   Yes

   ↓

2. Enrollment Agreement

   ↓

3. Admission Assessment

   ↓

   Core Services ————————→ No ——→ Further Assessment
                                    (Determine Enhanced/Intensive Services)

   ↓

   Yes ←————————————————————————————

   ↓

4. Written Plan of Care

   ↓

5. Care Plan Review and Assessment

   ↓

6. Coordination of Care

   ↓

7. Service Documentation

   ↓

8. Discharge Plan

PART FOUR: SERVICES

BACKGROUND

Traditionally, the key elements of adult day services have been the staff's interdisciplinary approaches to meeting participant goals; the therapeutic milieu; and the variety of services offered to meet the needs of participants. Adult day services differ from other forms of care in their unique focus on the strengths and abilities of participants, and on health rather than illness. Adult day services provide a structure to help people recover from an acute illness or injury, achieve rehabilitation, live with a chronic illness, maintain connections with their community, and/or use all of their retained skills.

The interaction of the physical and human environment combine to create the milieu of each center. The physical environment and the program design of adult day services provide safety and structure for participants. The center staff builds relationships and creates a culture that supports, involves, and validates the participant. This milieu then forms the framework in which therapeutic activities, health monitoring, and all the services offered by the center occur. All therapeutic components of adult day services (meals, activities, interactions with staff and other participants, personal care, nursing, and therapies) are reinforced by the warm, caring, affective tone of the center's milieu.

Adult day services have brought a new vocabulary and broader meaning to such familiar concepts as treatments and rehabilitation. From the beginning, the philosophy of adult day services has been that treatment and care alone were not enough. Concern with maximizing the quality of participants' lives mandates the holistic and interactive approach to services provided in adult day centers.

All individuals, groups, and centers are, of course, different. However, there are some commonly agreed upon principles of care that form the foundation for all services provided in a center.

- Routine is important for the participant, and following a regular daily schedule is a well-recognized means of providing needed structure.

- Sufficient flexibility to provide alternatives that accommodate unanticipated needs and events is necessary to maintain a calm and therapeutic milieu.

- All care is strength-based, with the staff compensating for the participants' losses and supporting the use of retained skills.

- Communication between staff and participants is the basis for creating a caring culture. This includes staff attending to the participants' verbal and nonverbal communication in order to understand their wants and needs, as well as staff using verbal and nonverbal means to validate and support participants.

- Sensitivity to all the elements of the participant's personality will convey a sense of respect that is the basis for forming supportive and therapeutic relationships.

THERAPEUTIC ACTIVITY

Background

Therapeutic activity is the glue that holds the adult day services program together.

A critical role of the center and staff is to build relationships and create a culture that supports, involves, and validates the participant. Therapeutic activity refers to that supportive culture and is a significant aspect of the individualized plan of care. A participant's activity includes everything the individual experiences during the day, not just arranged events.

As part of effective therapeutic activity the adult day program should:

- provide additional direction and support for the participant when needed, including, for example, breaking down activities into small, discrete steps or modeling behavior;

- have alternative programming available for any participants unable or unwilling to take part in a group activity; and

- explore and design activities that have the greatest potential to elicit a positive response from participants.

---

57 Programming shall take into consideration individual differences in age, health status, sensory deficits, life-style, ethnicity, religious affiliation, values, experiences, needs, interests, abilities, and skills by providing opportunities for a variety of types and levels of involvement.

Guidelines:
Activities may include, but are not limited to:
  - personal interaction;
  - activities naturally offered by the environment;
  - individualized activities;
  - small and large group activities;

- active and spectator participation;
- intergenerational experiences;
- involvement in community activities and events;
- services to individuals and to the program;
- outdoor activities as appropriate;
- self-care activities;
- food preparation and other IADL-related activities;
- culturally and ethnically diverse celebrations; and
- opportunities to voluntarily perform services for individuals and the program, and for community groups and organizations.

---

58 The activity plan shall be an integral part of the total plan of care for the individual based on the interest, needs, and abilities of the participant.

Guidelines:

Activities emphasize participants' strengths and abilities rather than impairments and contribute to participant feelings of competence and accomplishment. Provision is made for each individual to participate at his/her optimal level of functioning and to progress according to his/her own pace. Activity programming takes into account participants' individual responses to stimulation, level of fatigue, and tolerance for programming.

---

59 The adult day services program shall provide a balance of purposeful activities to meet the participants' interrelated needs and interests (social, intellectual, cultural, economic, emotional, physical, and spiritual).

Guideline:

These activities range from group and individual activities of general interest to specific therapeutic interventions—for example, creative arts therapies, wellness, prevention, and education.

---

60 Activities shall be designed to promote personal growth and enhance the self-image and/or to improve or maintain the functioning level of participants to the extent possible.

Guidelines:

Activities address the needs for security, control, inclusion, and affection. Activities offer, but are not limited to, opportunities to:

- preserve the participant's dignity;
- maximize remaining abilities;
- experience a positive outlet for energy, emotions, and self-expression;
- increase feelings of self-worth;
- maintain lifelong skills;
- learn new skills and gain knowledge;
- challenge and tap the potential abilities of participants;
- participate in activities of interest;
- improve capacity for independent functioning;
- develop interpersonal relationships;
- develop creative capacities;
- improve physical and emotional well-being, including nutritional status;
- be exposed to and involved in activities and events within the greater community;
- experience cultural enrichment; and
- have fun and enjoyable, pleasurable experiences.

61 Participants shall be encouraged to take part in activities, but may choose not to do so or may choose another activity.

Guidelines:

Centers should evaluate reasons for non-participation to determine whether it reflects personal preference or indicates a need for a change in activity.

Background noise such as conversation, television, microphone, or music can be therapeutic, distracting, or upsetting; therefore, centers should carefully assess the impact of noise on participants and make adjustments as indicated (for example, changing the type of music or volume level).

62 Participants shall be allowed time for rest and relaxation and to attend to personal and health care needs.

63 Activity opportunities shall be available whenever the center is in operation.

Guidelines:
A monthly calendar of activities can be prepared and posted in a visible place. This may be distributed to participants and family/caregivers and others. Group daily activities are posted in a prominent, convenient, visible place. Alternative simultaneous activities should be planned to allow optimum participant involvement.

ASSISTANCE WITH ADLs (formerly called Personal Care)

 64 The adult day services program shall provide assistance with and supervision of Activities of Daily Living (ADLs) in a safe and hygienic manner; with recognition of an individual's dignity and right to privacy; and in a manner that encourages the maximum level of independence.

Guidelines:
ADLs are defined as:

- Bathing—washing oneself by sponge bath or in either a tub or shower; bathing in a tub or shower includes the task of getting into or out of the tub or shower;

- Dressing—putting on and taking off all items of clothing and any necessary braces, fasteners, or artificial limbs;

- Eating—feeding oneself by getting food into the body from a receptacle (such as a plate, cup, or table) or by a feeding tube or intravenously;

- Toileting—getting to and from the toilet, getting on and off the toilet, and performing associated personal hygiene;

- Transferring—moving into or out of a bed, chair, or wheelchair;

- Mobility/ambulation—ability to walk with or without assistive devices or operate a wheel chair; and

- *Continence care—the ability to maintain control of bowel and bladder function; or when unable to maintain control of bowel or bladder function, the ability to perform associated personal hygiene (including the ability to care for catheter or colostomy).

Sometimes considered an ADL

Further direction on proper techniques for assisting with ADLs is available in the training materials: *A Manual for Training the Program Assistant in Adult Day Care* and the video, *Training the Program Assistant in Adult Day Care—Personal Care.*

In programs offering core services, assistance with ADLs may be provided by staff or trained volunteers—unless state law or regulations prohibit such help. At this level of care assistance is limited to providing a verbal or visual prompt to initiate the ADL. The participant must be able to complete the ADL independently.

In programs offering enhanced or intensive services, assistance with ADLs may be provided by staff or trained volunteers with clinical supervision available—unless prohibited by state law. As part of enhanced services, moderate assistance with 1-3 ADLs is provided. Moderate assistance includes standby or hands-on assistance throughout the completion of the ADL. As part of intensive services, either moderate assistance is provided with more than 3 ADLs, or one or more ADLs must be performed completely by staff.

HEALTH-RELATED SERVICES

Background
Health-related services promote health and wellness and evaluate the need for health interventions. They may enable the participant to experience improvement or to maintain his or her health status, but they may be unable to prevent inevitable decline. For some participants, supporting and facilitating current functioning are more appropriate than rehabilitation or restoration. Health care and nursing services, when appropriate, are included in health-related services.

 65 Health-related services, appropriate to the participants' needs, shall be offered by all adult day services programs.

Guidelines:
Health-related services may vary in intensity, depending on the need of the participants. Intensity is determined by both the number of participants requiring health-related services and the type of health-related services needed.

66

According to participant needs as identified in the health assessment, interdisciplinary plan of care, and physician orders, the health-related services shall include a configuration of services at different levels of intensity.

Core services:
Care requires persons trained in the skills necessary to provide health care coordination, prevention, and education as determined by the director or administrator of the program.

Enhanced services:
Health-related services may be provided by various health professionals within their permitted scope of practice. Medical/nursing services are provided by a part-time, full-time, or consulting nurse.

Intensive services:
Health-related services may be provided by various health professionals. Medical/nursing services are provided on a full-time basis by a licensed nurse.

67

Health-related services are to be provided at all ranges of care. All adult day services programs shall:
- Refer to and assist with coordination of other health services, as needed;
- Train staff and supervise use of standard protocols for communicable diseases and infection control;
- Provide emergency first aid and initiate emergency response procedures. This must be provided by a person trained in Emergency First Aid and CPR; and
- Provide or arrange for health education, promotion, prevention, screening, and detection.

68

All centers shall monitor health.

Core services:
Adult day services observe each participant's physical and mental well-being and take appropriate action as needed, according to predetermined protocols.

Enhanced services:
Enhanced services involve providing intermittent monitoring and intervention for ongoing medical conditions, including vital signs and weight, and providing observation, monitoring, and intervention for changes in cognitive or physical conditions or functional level.

Intensive services:
The intensive services level involves providing ongoing monitoring and intervention for acute or continuing medical conditions, including vital signs and weight, and providing observation, monitoring, and intervention for cognitive, physical, or functional changes.

---

69 All adult day centers shall coordinate care.

Core services:
Adult day services advise and monitor contact by the participant and/or family/caregiver with participant's primary care physician and others involved in care.

Enhanced or intensive services:
At the enhanced or intensive level a licensed nurse will monitor, coordinate care and, if needed, contact the participant's primary care physician.

---

70 All adult day centers shall provide health care.

Core services:
Adult day services collect, maintain, and update—within the scope of practice of the staff involved—medical and functional information and assessments. For those areas outside of the scope of practice of the staff involved, the center maintains a file and notifies others when assessments and other medical and functional reports are due.

Enhanced services:
Enhanced services involve providing restorative, supportive, or rehabilitative care that includes assessment, monitoring, and intervention on a moderate and intermittent basis for ongoing medical conditions and functional limitations.

Intensive services:
The intensive services level involves providing skilled nursing services that are within the scope of practice permitted and that can safely be done at the center to observe and manage medical conditions according to physician orders.

---

71   All adult day centers offering enhanced and intensive services shall manage medication.

Core services:
Adult day services programs offering core services maintain medication information. They also provide reminders or prompt the participant to initiate and follow through with self-administration of medications.

Enhanced services:
Enhanced services programs provide training in self-administration of medications or administering medications. Centers regularly inspect drug inventory and storage conditions. They evaluate the potential for drug interactions and side effects. Centers evaluate how the home situation fosters or impedes the ability to procure, store, and appropriately administer or self-administer medications. They establish drug review with the primary responsible party and the physician, and also monitor and evaluate participants receiving enteral tube feedings.

Intensive services:
These services include providing intravenous, intramuscular, or subcutaneous injections by trained and licensed staff.

---

72   Adult day centers offering enhanced and intensive services shall provide nursing services.

Core services:
At this level centers are not required to provide nursing services.

Enhanced services:
At this level centers provide other direct nursing services requiring intermittent skilled nursing. They supervise or provide maintenance therapy procedures and provide written and verbal

instructions to staff, participants, and the family/caregiver on the diagnosis and treatment protocol of the participant. They also document instruction provided to the participant and/or family/caregiver.

Intensive services:
These include full-time nursing services and specialty nursing care such as medical or psychiatric nursing treatment and care.

SOCIAL SERVICES

> **73** Social services shall be provided to participants and their families. Staff shall assess the families' needs and assist them in gaining access to additional services as needed.

Guideline:
These services include support groups, in-home care, residential placement, and counseling.

> **74** Staff shall provide to participants and their families/caregiver education and support on issues jointly agreed upon.

Guidelines:
According to participant needs as identified in the social assessment and interdisciplinary plan of care, social services may include a configuration of the following responsibilities, depending on the level of intensity needed.

For participants with a progressive disease, the staff continually assesses the participants' and families' needs and helps families gain access to additional services needed.

Core services:
For participants receiving core services who have identified problems or needs not met by the center, programs provide for referral to community services.

Enhanced and intensive services:

For centers serving individuals receiving enhanced or intensive services, the center:

- provides counseling to participants and families/caregivers, facilitating the participant's adaptation to the adult day services programs and active involvement in the plan of care, if appropriate;

- arranges for other community services not provided by the adult day services center and works with these agencies to coordinate all services;

- serves as participant advocate by asserting and safeguarding the human and civil rights of the participant;

- assesses for signs of mental illness and/or dementia and makes appropriate referrals;

- provides information and referral for persons not appropriate for adult day services;

- provides family conferences, serves as liaison between participant, family/caregiver, and center;

- provides individual or group counseling and support to caregivers and participants;

- conducts support groups or facilitates participant or family/caregiver participation in support groups; and

- assists staff in adapting to changes in participants' behavior.

Intensive services:

For centers with participants who receive intensive services and who have significant psychosocial needs, care may include providing or arranging for individual, group, or family psychotherapy. Under the direction of social services staff, the staff may use behavioral interventions to improve participants' adaptation to the therapeutic setting.

FOOD SERVICES

> **75** All adult day programs shall provide participants with a minimum of one meal per day of an adult's daily nutritional requirement as established by state and federal regulations.

Guidelines:

Snacks and fluids will be offered as appropriate to meet the participants' nutritional and fluid needs. All foods offered will be nutritious, appetizing, and safe. The program will respect dietary restrictions related to religion or culture and will offer ethnically appropriate foods whenever feasible.

The participant's total dietary intake is of concern but is not the center's responsibility. The center is responsible only for meals served at the center.

76	Liberalized diets shall be encouraged. However, special, modified, or therapeutic diets shall be provided as necessary for participants with medical conditions or functional impairments.

Guidelines:

"Special," "modified," or "therapeutic" diets are terms that are often used interchangeably to designate diets prescribed by a physician, which may include modifications in nutrient content, caloric value, consistency or texture, methods of food preparation, or a combination of these modifications. The most common forms of these diets are diabetic (or low simple sugar), low salt (or low sodium), vegetarian, and texture modifications (such as ground, pureed, or mechanical soft).

Special, modified, or therapeutic diets ordered by the participant's physician are included in the interdisciplinary plan of care.

77	An adult day services program shall neither admit nor continue to serve a participant whose dietary requirements cannot be accommodated by the center.

NUTRITION SERVICES

Background

Nutrition services are designed to improve participants' nutritional and physical status, independence, and quality of life, and to prevent further deterioration unless otherwise unavoidable. Nutrition therapy consists of screening and assessing participants for risk or presence of poor nutritional status; developing and implementing an appropriate plan of care to achieve the goals of the participant, family/caregiver, and interdisciplinary team; and monitoring and evaluating the plan.

---

78 All adult day services programs shall screen and assess participants for nutrition therapy needs and shall provide nutrition intervention as appropriate.

Core services:
Nutrition services will consist of screening participants for nutritional well-being and providing general nutrition education to participants and families/caregivers. Nutrition screening and education may be the responsibility of a dietetic professional, the administrator, or program director.

Enhanced and intensive services:
Nutrition services as part of enhanced and intensive services consist of screening and assessing the nutritional health of participants and developing a nutrition plan of care consistent with the goals established by the participant, family/caregiver, and interdisciplinary team, including the participant's physician. Nutrition assessment and plan of care development, implementation, and monitoring are the responsibility of a Registered Dietitian (RD), Dietetic Technician Registered (DTR), RD- or DTR-eligible, or other health care professional, consistent with state licensure laws.

Nutrition therapy services, which include but are not limited to the following, will:

- assess a participant's nutritional health via dietary history evaluation, anthropometric measures, laboratory tests and/or physical parameters, and medical history;

- evaluate potential for interactions between nutrients, drugs, and foods that may adversely affect the nutritional and health status of the participant;

- evaluate how the home situation fosters or hinders the ability to procure, store, prepare, and/or consume food;

- establish a nutritional plan of care to prevent participant's deterioration and achieve optimal nutritional health;

- evaluate and redesign the nutritional plan of care as necessary;

- monitor and evaluate participants receiving enteral tube feedings and parenteral line solutions, and recommend changes as appropriate;

- provide written and verbal instructions to staff, participant, and family/caregiver to achieve optimal nutritional health;

- teach and train staff in foods, nutrition, and nutrition therapy; and

- provide additional nutrition therapy services as needed.

TRANSPORTATION

79 The adult day program shall provide, arrange, or contract for transportation to enable persons, including persons with disabilities, to attend the center and to participate in center-sponsored outings.

80 The adult day program shall have a transportation policy that includes routine and emergency procedures, with a copy of the relevant procedures located in all vehicles.

Guideline:
Accidents, medical emergencies, weather emergencies, and escort issues should be addressed.

81 All center vehicles shall be equipped with a device for two-way communication.

82 All program-provided and contracted transportation systems shall meet local, state, and federal regulations.

Participants should be transported for no more than sixty minutes without the opportunity for a rest stop.

EMERGENCY CARE FOR PARTICIPANTS

83 The center shall have a written procedure for handling medical emergencies.

Guidelines:
This document should include:
- procedure for notification;
- transportation arrangements; and
- provision for an escort, if necessary.

84 The center shall have a portable basic emergency information file available on each client that includes:
-hospital preference;
-physician of record and telephone number;
-emergency contact (family);
-insurance information;
-medications/allergies;
-current diagnosis and history; and
-photograph (for participant identification).

85 The center shall have a written procedure for responding to participant development.

Guidelines:
This procedure describes:
- staff responsibilities;
- notification protocols; and
- photograph (for participant identification).

EDUCATION

 Education shall be provided to the families/caregivers and participants to improve the well-being and functional level of the participants and/or caregiver.

Guidelines:
Education includes health teaching, nutrition, housing, services and benefits available, and legal and financial planning.

Education is an ongoing process that is both formal and informal.

ANCILLARY SERVICES

Ancillary services include traditional professional therapies, creative arts, wellness services, and expanded educational services. Ancillary services are provided to help participants achieve their optimal level of functioning

Background

The following services may be provided directly or through contractual arrangements by an adult day program when appropriate and when needed by participants and staff. The scope and intensity of these services will vary depending upon the needs of the participants and/or staff and the range of care provided.

87 Ancillary services shall be procured to meet needs identified through the assessment and care plan process.

88 Ancillary services shall include education for the participant and/or family caregiver and/or staff and may be delivered on a one-to-one or group basis.

89 Ancillary services shall be provided within the framework of the individualized plan of care and as part of the overall array of services the participant receives.

90 Professional therapy services may address remediation but shall also focus on adaptive and compensatory techniques.

91 Centers providing services defined by professional practice standards shall ensure that these standards are met.

92 Physical, occupational, and speech therapy services shall be provided directly or through contracted or other arrangements by an adult day program when appropriate and when needed by participants.

93 The scope and intensity of these services shall vary depending upon the needs of the participants and the range of services provided.

PHYSICAL THERAPY

Physical therapy services are provided to restore or maintain maximum mobility, lower extremity function, and muscle function.

Core services:
At this level centers are not required to provide physical therapy services.

Enhanced services:
The adult day services program provides or arranges for physical therapy services at a functional maintenance level—based on the physical therapy assessment, interdisciplinary plan of care, and physician orders.

Physical therapy services, which include but are not limited to the following, will:

- assess participant's mobility level, strength, range of motion, endurance, balance, gait, ability to transfer, coordination, posture, and pain level;

- provide treatment to relieve pain and/or develop, restore, maintain functioning;

- establish a functional maintenance program and provide written and verbal instructions to center staff and the family/caregiver to assist the participant with implementation;

- recommend adaptive or assistive devices;

- train other staff to lift, move, and otherwise assist participants;

- evaluate the home setting for environmental barriers and make recommendations for increased participant independence; and

- assist participants to obtain assistive ambulatory devices and train participants and family/caregivers in the proper use of the device.

Intensive services:
The adult day services program offering this range provides or arranges for all of the enhanced services and will also provide restorative or rehabilitative therapy when indicated.

OCCUPATIONAL THERAPY

Occupational therapy services are provided to restore independence in activities of daily living, facilitate ease of caregiving, and maintain community integration.

Core services:
At this level centers are not required to provide occupational therapy services.

Enhanced services:
The adult day services program provides or arranges for occupational therapy services at a functional maintenance level, based upon the occupational therapy assessment, interdisciplinary plan of care, and physician orders. Occupational therapy services, which include but are not limited to the following, will:

- administer diagnostic and prognostic tests to determine the integrity of upper extremities, ability to transfer, range of motion, balance, strength and coordination, endurance, activities of daily living, and cognitive-perceptual functioning;

- teach participants adaptive techniques to overcome barriers and impediments to activities of daily living;

- teach and train other staff in the use of therapeutic, creative, and self-care activities to improve or maintain the participant's capacity for self-care and independence, and increase the range of motion, strength, and coordination;

- train the participant in the use of supportive and adaptive equipment and assistive devices;

- evaluate the home for environmental barriers and recommend changes needed for greater participant independence;

- establish and monitor functional maintenance programs to prevent deterioration, and provide written and verbal instructions to center staff and the family/caregiver to assist the participant with implementation; and

- provide other appropriate occupational therapy procedures.

Intensive services:
The adult day services program offering this range provides or arranges for all of the enhanced services and will also provide restorative or rehabilitative therapy when indicated.

SPEECH THERAPY

Speech therapy services are provided to treat swallowing problems and to restore impaired speech and language functions.

Core services:
At this level centers are not required to provide speech therapy services.

Enhanced services:
The adult day services program provides or arranges for speech therapy services at a functional maintenance level, based upon the speech therapy assessment, plan of care, and physician orders. Speech therapy services, which include but are not limited to the following, will:

- establish a treatment program to improve communication ability and correct disorders;

- provide written and verbal instructions to center staff and family/caregivers in methods to assist the participant to improve and correct speech disorders;

- provide swallowing assessment and, if participant is at risk, then include appropriate precautions in the interdisciplinary plan of care and provide education and information to participant (if appropriate) and to family/caregiver; and

- provide additional speech therapy services as needed.

Intensive services:
The adult day services program provides or arranges for all of the enhanced services and will also:
- provide appropriate services to participants assessed at high risk for choking; and
- provide restorative or rehabilitative speech therapy when indicated.

CREATIVE ARTS THERAPIES

Background

Many of the assessment processes and treatment goals are shared by two or more of the creative arts therapies. However, the specific methods used vary according to the modality (music, art, or dance/movement). Because the needs, abilities, and interests of participants are diverse, the different creative arts therapies make it possible to meet those needs in a variety of ways. Often, these therapies are appropriately combined with other therapies for increased effectiveness.

94 The creative arts therapies shall be provided in order to improve or maintain physical, cognitive, or social functioning.

Guidelines:
Music therapy is the controlled use of music in the treatment, rehabilitation, education, and training of individuals with physical, mental, and emotional disorders. Dance/movement

therapy uses movement as a process that furthers the emotional, cognitive, and physical integration of the individual. Art therapy uses participant responses to art media and images to reflect an individual's development, abilities, personality, interests, concerns, and conflicts.

Music, art, and/or dance/movement therapy services include, but are not limited to, the following tasks:
- assessing the participant's physical/motor functioning (including mobility, strength, endurance, coordination, balance, and level of pain), sensory/perceptual abilities, communication skills, cognitive functioning, ability to remember and/or follow instructions, social history, and past and present abilities and the ability to benefit from the creative arts;
- developing an individual treatment plan based on identified need(s);
- implementing therapy treatment plans in order to promote such benefits as:
  - increases in muscle strength, range of motion, improvement or maintenance of large and small motor function, circulation, and active participation in exercise activities;
  - exploration of mental health needs;
  - alleviation or adaptation to chronic pain;
  - alleviation of loneliness and isolation, increased social confidence and self-esteem;
  - elevation of mood;
  - enhanced ability to express feelings and emotions;
  - adopting alternative methods of communication;
  - relaxation and reduction of stress, agitation, depression, or catastrophic behaviors;
  - discovery or rediscovery of talents;
  - decrease in pain, increase in emotional support and comfort;
  - learning of new skills and concepts; and
  - evaluation and redesigning of programs, as necessary.

MEDICAL SERVICES

95 Each participant shall have a physician responsible for his or her care. The physician of record shall be clearly identified in the participant's chart.

96 The center shall have a policy regarding the provision of medical services in relation to participant care.

Guidelines:
Centers may have a physician or other qualified health care provider who serves as a consultant to the interdisciplinary team, and authorizes the plan of care. The physician may also serve as medical director or directly provide hands-on assessment and/or treatment if authorized by the participant's primary care provider. Medical services may also be provided by the participant's personal physician, who may participate in the development of the plan of care and is contacted when changes or emergencies occur, provides medical assessment and treatment, is regularly informed of the participant's status, and retains primary responsibility for medical care. In centers where a medical director or consultant is available to act as a member of the team and authorize care, information is usually supplied to the personal physician, who may still provide the ongoing medical treatment.

OPTIONAL SERVICES

The following services are not required of all centers. They may be provided directly or through contractual arrangements by an adult day center if appropriate for the center and needed by the participants: dentistry; laboratory, radiological and diagnostic services; pharmacy; psychiatry/psychology; podiatry; ophthalmology/optometry; audiology; and others. Services may range from consultation to prescription of assistive devices, to ongoing treatment. The scope and intensity of these services will vary, depending upon the needs of the participants and the program of the center. Generally, these services will not be provided as part of the core services.

All optional health-related services provided by the center shall meet the following general standards:
- the provider shall meet state requirements for licensure or certification where applicable;
- space for privacy shall be provided by the center;
- special equipment shall be available when necessary;
- if these services are provided at another location by contract with the adult day center, the adult day center shall be responsible for arranging or providing transportation and escort services if needed;
- the provider shall document all services rendered in the participant's medical chart;
- laboratory, radiological, and diagnostic results shall be entered in the participant's record when available; and
- authorization and approval for payment of services shall be identified.

OTHER OPTIONAL SERVICES

| 98 | Any other services offered in the center shall meet applicable state, local, and professional requirements. |

Guideline:
Such services may include, for example, those of a cosmetologist or barber.

PART FIVE: STAFFING

BACKGROUND

It is important that staff members possess certain personality traits and attitudes. Many of these qualities—such as commitment, empathy, patience, flexibility, and a sense of humor—are common to staff in all adult day service programs. Staff members must always have energy and enthusiasm for their work, but they also need to project a feeling of calmness. The staff must be interested in and concerned for the participants and sensitive to their special needs. They should want to help people and to engage them in meaningful activities that are fun and creative, yet age-appropriate. They must also respect people for who they are and accept individual strengths and abilities without unrealistic expectations for improvement.

The center's employment criteria should be flexible enough to consider the applications of individuals who are open to learning and have a genuine interest in working with special populations. It is often more difficult to retrain someone who has learned an approach that is inappropriate for the program than it is to take someone with no experience and train him/her.

Staff who remain in this field are generally perseverant and optimistic. They derive their greatest satisfaction not from the progress they see but from the happiness and enjoyment found in the day center experience and from the positive impact they have on the participants' and family/caregivers' quality of life.

99	Staff shall be adequate in number and skills to provide essential administrative and service functions.

Guideline:
Staff also should be sufficient to:
- serve the number and functioning levels of adult day service participants;
- meet program objectives; and
- provide access to other community resources.

STAFF-PARTICIPANT RATIO

---

100   There shall be at least two (2) responsible persons (one a paid staff member) at the center at all times when there are two or more participants in attendance.

Intent:
Staff included in the staff-participant ratio should include only those who work on site, are actively involved with the participants, and are immediately available to meet participants' needs.

---

101   The staff-participant ratio shall be sufficient to meet the needs of the participants in attendance.

Guideline:
It is recommended that the staff-participant ratio be a minimum of one to six (1:6) in a program offering core services.

---

102   As the number of participants with functional impairments increases or the severity of the impairment increases, the staff-participant ratio shall be adjusted accordingly.

Guidelines:
Programs serving a high percentage of participants who are severely impaired should consider a staff-participant ratio of one to four (1:4) when providing enhanced and/or intensive services.

In programs serving more than 20 participants, the center may find that an overall staff ratio of 1:5 is sufficient when providing enhanced and/or intensive services.

103 If the administrator is responsible for more than one site or has duties not directly related to adult day services, a program director shall be designated for each additional site. (See also "Part Two: Administration and Organization," page 21.) In the absence of the director, a staff member shall be designated to supervise the center.

104 To ensure continuity of care, adequate quality, and safety of participants, centers shall provide for qualified substitute staff.

105 Volunteers shall be included in the staff ratio ONLY WHEN THEY CONFORM TO THE SAME STANDARDS AND REQUIREMENTS AS PAID STAFF, meet the job qualification standards of the organization, and have designated responsibilities, as permitted by state or local licensing requirements.

106 Each center that is co-located with another, non-adult day services program in the same facility shall have its own staff with hours that are committed to the adult day services program.

BASIC REQUIREMENTS FOR ALL STAFF

The requirements in this section are relevant to all employed staff and to volunteers serving as staff.

107 Each staff member shall be competent and qualified for the position held.

108

References shall be checked and job histories verified for all staff and volunteers serving as staff.

Guideline:
If state law permits, a check of abuse registries and criminal histories, finger-printing, and a drug screening are recommended.

109

Each staff member shall have had a physical examination, including tuberculosis screening, within twelve (12) months prior to employment, and a copy of the report of the examination shall be filed in personnel records within 30 days of employment. Agency personnel policies shall also specify the intervals at which future physical examinations are required. Volunteers shall have tuberculosis screening—except those who are not acting in the capacity of staff.

110

Staff and volunteers shall sign a confidentiality agreement and hold all information about participants and families in confidence, treating all participants with respect and dignity.

111

All direct service staff shall have input into the plan of care and ongoing assessment for each participant for whom they have responsibility, carrying out the objectives for the participant and performing other services as required. (See "Plan of Care", page 37)

112

Staff members shall follow an established system for daily communication to ensure ongoing transmittal of pertinent information among staff.

113	Staff responsibilities and functions shall cross staff disciplinary lines, and the staff shall function as a team for the good and well-being of the participants.

STAFF TRAINING AND EVALUATION

114	Staff shall have adequate skills, education, and experience to serve the population in a manner consistent with the philosophy of the adult day center.

Guidelines:

All staff and volunteers who have contact with and responsibility for special populations should receive specific training in serving that population, conducted by a qualified trainer or facilitated by a trained staff member.

Staff and volunteers should reflect the ethnic and cultural background of the community and the adult day center participants.

115	All personnel, paid and volunteer, shall be provided training.

Guidelines:
- General orientation includes, but is not limited to:
    - purpose and goals of adult day services;
    - roles and responsibilities of other staff members;
    - behavioral interventions/behavior acceptance/accommodation;
    - health, Universal Precautions;
    - information on fire and safety measures/codes;
    - philosophy of the program and parent organization;
    - confidentiality;
    - interdisciplinary team approach;
    - participant rights;

- needs of target population (for example, those with dementia or developmental disability);
- depression;
- medication management;
- the center's policies and regulations;
- communication skills;
- review of basic terminology;
- advance directive policies;
- elder abuse reporting;
- how to safely and appropriately help participants perform ADLs (including good body mechanics); and
- risk management.

Ongoing training includes at least four (4) in-service training sessions per year to enhance quality of care and job performance. At the time of employment, and annually, each employee must receive training in:
- needs of the participants in the center's target population;
- infection control;
- fire, safety, disaster plan, and the center's emergency plan;
- choking prevention and intervention techniques;
- body mechanics/transfer techniques/assistance with ADLs;
- mandatory reporting laws of abuse/neglect;
- basics of nutritional care, food safety, and safe feeding techniques;
- CPR and first aid, as appropriate (See also "Part Two: Administration and Organization," page 21); and
- behavioral intervention/behavior acceptance/accommodation.
- There should also be opportunities for additional education, depending on the resources of the agency.

---

116   There shall be timely evaluations of staff members.

Guidelines:
- a written evaluation of the introductory period of employment (signed by the employee) should take place no later than at the end of the first six months of employment; and
- a written performance evaluation should occur at least annually, use a standardized instrument, and involve a face-to-face meeting.

STAFF POSITIONS

Background

Not every program needs a large interdisciplinary team. Certain minimum staffing requirements, however, can be defined in terms of services provided. Some services cannot be delivered by those without professional training. This does not mean that all staff members must have such qualifications, but it does mean that the center must have the proper balance of professionals and paraprofessionals or nonprofessionals to adequately meet the needs of participants. The list in this section is intended as a guide to staff qualifications and responsibilities; it is not intended to provide detailed descriptions. Staff selection depends on participant needs, program design, and regulatory requirements.

If an individual performs more than one role, then he or she must be qualified for both positions.

Some positions may be provided as an in-kind contribution (for example, the custodian) or as a contracted service (for example, a driver provided when transportation is contracted).

Even if it has been determined that a paraprofessional can accomplish a specific task, a professional must be responsible for the development and supervision of services. It is necessary to consider and meet state and federal regulations for professional services.

THE CREDENTIALS SPECIFIED IN THE BRIEF DESCRIPTIONS BELOW ARE THOSE PREFERRED. PLEASE NOTE THAT THE DISCUSSION OF PROGRAM FLEXIBILITY IN THE INTRODUCTION APPLIES TO THE POSITIONS AND CREDENTIALS.

ADMINISTRATOR (may also be known as executive director, CEO, or president).

 There shall be a qualified administrator responsible for the development, coordination, supervision, fiscal management, and evaluation of services provided through the adult day services program.

Guidelines:
The administrator should have a master's degree and one year supervisory experience (full-time or equivalent) or bachelor's degree and three years supervisory experience in a social or health service setting--or comparable technical and human service training with demonstrated competence and experience as a manager in a health or human service setting.

Depending on the size and structure of the organization, some duties may be delegated to other staff. Sample duties may include the following:
- developing administrative policies and procedures;
- developing resources for the center, including fund-raising, grant writing, budget development, and fiscal monitoring;
- ensuring compliance with licensing and funding regulations;
- facilitating and organizing advocacy efforts;
- assessing the center's progress in accordance with established goals and objectives and a quality assurance plan;
- implementing board policies; and
- hiring and supervising staff.

PROGRAM DIRECTOR (also known as center manager, site manager, center coordinator—may also be the administrator).

118	The program director shall organize, implement, and coordinate the daily operation of the adult day services program in accordance with participants' needs and any mandatory requirements, under the direction of the administrator.

Guidelines:
The program director should have a bachelor's degree in health or social services or a related field, with one year supervisory experience (full-time or equivalent) in a social or health service setting—or comparable technical and human service training with demonstrated competence and experience as a manager in a health or human service setting.

Sample duties may include supervision of, or direct responsibility for, the following:
- planning the day services program to meet individual needs of the participants, liaison with community agencies, and providing services to individuals and families when necessary;
- coordinating the development and ongoing review and monitoring of each participant's individual plan of care, and making necessary program adjustments;
- establishment, maintenance, and monitoring of internal management systems to facilitate scheduling and coordination of services, and for the collection of pertinent participant data;
- recruitment, hiring, and general supervision of all staff, volunteers, and contractors;
- training and utilization of volunteers with consideration of their individual talents; and
- program activities to work effectively with the day services program.

71

It is recommended that all directors and administrators complete the NADSA training course and the NADSA certification process to be Certified Directors or Administrators in Adult Day Services.

SOCIAL WORKER

> **119** There shall be a designated, qualified social service staff person.

Guidelines:
The social worker should have a master's degree in social work and at least one year of professional work experience (full-time or the equivalent), or a bachelor's degree in social work and two years of experience, or a bachelor's degree in another field and two years experience in a human service field. If licensure is required by the state, then the social worker must comply with licensure requirements.

Depending on the setting and licensing requirements, these functions may be performed by other human services professionals, such as rehabilitation counselors, gerontologists, or mental health workers, (although they may not call themselves social workers without appropriate credentials). (The duties of the social worker are included in "Part Four: Services, Social Services," page 50.)

NURSE

> **120** For programs offering nursing services: the nurse shall be a Registered Nurse (RN) with valid state credentials and a minimum of one year applicable experience (full-time or equivalent).

Guidelines:
It is preferable that the experience has involved working with the aging and adults with chronic impairments and that all or part of the experience has been in a community health setting. It is also preferable that the nurse have a B.S.N. (The duties of the nurse are described in "Part Four: Services, Health-Related Services," pages 46-50.)

In addition, the nurse often provides services that would be provided by another professional staff member if that staff member were a full-time employee (for example, services provided by the physical therapist). *

In programs providing Core Services a nurse is not required.

ACTIVITIES COORDINATOR

121
For programs providing Core Services:
The activities coordinator shall have a high school diploma or the equivalent plus one year of experience in developing and conducting activities for the population to be served in the program.

For programs providing Enhanced and Intensive Services:
The activities coordinator shall have a bachelor's degree plus one year of experience (full-time or equivalent) in developing and conducting activities for the population to be served or an associate's degree in a related field plus two years of appropriate experience.

Guidelines:
It is preferred that the degree include a major in recreation, occupational therapy, the arts, humanities, social, or health services and that experience include therapeutic recreation for older adults and those with a disability.

The activities coordinator shall be responsible for planning, conducting, and supervising the therapeutic activities offered, as described in "Part Four: Services, Therapeutic Activities," pages 42-45.

In addition, the activities coordinator should arrange for consultation with certified or licensed therapists in creative arts.

PROGRAM ASSISTANT

122
The program assistant shall have a high school diploma or the equivalent and one or more years of experience in working with adults in a health care or social service setting. In addition, the program assistant shall have received training in working with older adults and in conducting activities for the population to be served.

Guidelines:
Under certain circumstances, completion of training and an internship may be substituted for work experience.

Program assistants should complete the NADSA training course and the NADSA certification process to be Certified Program Assistants in Adult Day Services.

Duties may include:
- providing personal care and assistance to participants;
- working with other staff members as required in implementing and carrying out services and activities and in meeting the needs of individual participants; and
- assisting with transportation of and escorting participants to, from, and within the center, if appropriate.

THERAPISTS

123 Physical therapists, occupational therapists, speech therapists, dietetic/medical nutrition therapists, recreation therapists, mental health therapists, and any other therapists utilized shall have valid state credentials and one year of experience in a social or health setting.

Creative arts therapists (professionals providing art, music, drama, and dance/movement therapy) shall have completed appropriate college-level and clinical training. They shall also be certified by the appropriate national professional organization in their field.

Guideline:
Therapies may be provided by staff of the center or through contracts.

FOOD SERVICE DIRECTOR

124 If the adult day services program prepares its own food on site, there shall be a food service director.

Guidelines:
This director should be a Registered Dietitian (R.D.), Dietetic Technician Registered (D.T.R.), R.D. - or D.T.R. - eligible, or a graduate of a four-year baccalaureate program in

nutrition/dietetics/food service and should have one or more years of experience in working with adults in a health care or social service setting.

Duties may include:
- food ordering, procurement, preparation, safety, and service;
- providing nutrition-related services including nutrition screening; nutrition assessment; care plan development, implementation, and evaluation; and discharge; and
- policy and procedure development related to food and nutrition services.

If food is not prepared on site, the administrator or program director will assume responsibility for food service operations.

If licensure is required by the state for one or more of these duties, then the food service director must comply with licensure requirements. (See "Food Services and Nutrition" in "Part Four: Services," pages 51-54)

CONSULTANTS AND CONTRACT EMPLOYEES

125 Consultants shall be available to provide services as needed in order to supplement professional staff and enhance the program's quality.

Guideline:
Consulting services may be provided by contractual agreement with community groups or on an individual basis. Examples include legal, nutrition, business and financial management; psychiatric and medical; physical, occupational, speech, and creative arts therapy; pharmacy; and therapeutic recreation.

SECRETARY/BOOKKEEPER

126 The secretary/bookkeeper shall have at least a high school diploma or equivalent and skills and training to carry out the duties of the position.

Guidelines:
Duties may include:
- assisting in developing and maintaining a record-keeping system for the program;
- performing tasks necessary to handle correspondence and office activities;

- answering the telephone in a courteous and informative manner; and
- bookkeeping, maintaining of financial records, and billing for services.

DRIVER

> **127** The driver shall have a valid and appropriate state driver's license, a safe driving record, and training in first aid and CPR (cardiopulmonary resuscitation). The driver shall meet any state requirements for licensure or certification.

Guidelines:
The driver, who could also be a program assistant in the center, should be aware of basic transfer techniques and safe ambulation. Experience in assisting older adults and adults with impairments is desirable, as is the successful completion of a defensive driving course, training in sensitivity to the needs of older adults, and, where appropriate, passenger assistance training. Sample duties may include:
- providing round trip transportation from participant home to center, and providing escort service as needed to ensure participant safety;
- ensuring that all appropriate safety measures are carried out while transporting participants; and
- reporting behavioral changes or unusual incidents involving participants to appropriate professional staff and consulting with other program staff as necessary.

VOLUNTEERS

> **128** The center shall keep a record of volunteer hours/activities and provide appropriate recognition of volunteers.

> **129** The volunteers shall be individuals or groups who want to work with adult day service participants and shall take part in program orientation and training. The duties of volunteers shall be mutually determined by volunteers and staff. Duties, to be performed under the supervision of a staff member, shall either supplement staff in established activities or provide additional services for which the volunteer has special talents.

Guidelines:

Sample duties may include:
- working under the direction of paid program and professional staff, carrying out program activities;
- providing supplemental activities (such as parties and special events);
- fund-raising and assisting in public relations; and
- leading activities in areas of special knowledge, experience, or expertise.

PART SIX: FACILITY

BACKGROUND

The physical environment of the adult day center has great potential as a therapeutic tool. A well-planned environment has the appropriate supports and cues to enhance the participants' ability to function as independently as possible and to engage in program activities. The environment plays an even more significant role as an individual's level of impairment increases. There is no single "best design" or "perfect environment," but creativity and imagination are two key factors in producing an effective environmental design.

A center needs to be pleasant, comfortable, and safe.

In designing an adult day center, planners must create an environment that supports the principles of adult day services and will:
- promote the safety of each participant and staff;
- maximize the functional level of the participant and encourage independence to the greatest degree possible;
- build on the participants' strengths, while recognizing their limitations and impairments;
- establish for the participant a sense of control and self-determination, regardless of his/her level of functioning; and
- assist in maintaining the physical and emotional health of the participant while preventing further debilitation whenever possible.

The environment is critically important. The physical modifications listed here will have an impact on the experience of participants with cognitive and functional impairments, but it is the overall environment—created by the physical plant and appropriate adaptations; staff skills, attitudes, and demeanor; and therapeutic activity that is key to maintaining a positive and supportive setting that enables each individual to function successfully at the highest possible level.

SPACE

| 130 | The facility shall comply with applicable state and local building regulations, and zoning, fire, and health codes or ordinances. The facility shall also comply with the requirements of the Americans with Disabilities Act of 1990. |

Guidelines:

Some states require compliance with ANSI Standard A117.1-1980; "Specification for Making Buildings and Facilities Accessible to and Usable by Physically Handicapped People," is recommended as an excellent guide.

When possible, the facility should be located on the street level. If the center is not located at street level, it is essential to have a ramp and/or elevators.

131	Each adult day center, when it is co-located in a facility housing other services, shall have its own separate identifiable space for main activity areas during operational hours.

Guideline:

Certain space, such as the kitchen and therapy rooms, can be shared.

132	The facility shall provide at least sixty (60) square feet of program space for multipurpose use for each day service participant.

Intent:

The facility needs sufficient space to accommodate the full range of program activities, services, and equipment. The facility should be flexible and adaptable to accommodate variations of activities (group and/or individual) and services and to protect the privacy of participants receiving services.

Guidelines:

It is strongly recommended that centers serving a significant number of people with cognitive impairment or those who use adaptive equipment for ambulation or medical care provide eighty to one hundred (80 - 100) square feet per participant.

In determining adequate square footage, only those activity areas commonly used by participants are to be included. Dining and kitchen areas are to be included only if these areas are used by participants for activities other than meals. Reception areas, storage areas, offices, restrooms, passageways, treatment rooms, service areas, or specialized spaces used only for therapies are not to be included when calculating square footage.

133 There shall be sufficient private space to permit staff to work effectively and without interruption.

Intent:
The stress of providing adult day services is high, and environmental supports are essential to assist staff members to maintain good staff morale and job satisfaction.

Guideline:
In addition, it is highly recommended that staff have a separate restroom and separate eating place.

134 There shall be an identified separate space available for participants and/or family/caregivers to have private discussions with staff.

135 There shall be storage space for program and operating supplies.

136 The center's restrooms shall be located as near the activity area as possible.

Guideline:
It is preferable that the restrooms be no more than forty (40) feet away from the activity area.

137 The facility shall include at least one toilet for every ten (10) participants.

Guidelines:
Programs that have a large number of participants that require more scheduled toileting or assistance with toileting should have at least one toilet for every eight (8) participants. The toilets should be equipped for use by persons with limited mobility, easily accessible from all program areas, designed to allow assistance from one or two staff, and barrier-free.

If there is a medical clinic/health treatment room in the facility, it is highly recommended that there also be an adjacent bathroom with a shower accessible to those with a disability.

Some participants may be incontinent. Arrangements can be made with the family/caregiver to leave at least one extra set of clothing at the center. If laundry services are available on site, and if staff time is available, soiled clothing may be washed at the center.

---

138 The facility shall have a rest area for participants.

Guideline:
This designated area permits privacy and isolates participants who become ill or disruptive, or who require rest. It should be separate from activities areas, near a restroom, and supervised.

---

139 Space shall be available for the safe arrival and departure of participants.

Guideline:
It is recommended that there be sufficient, lighted parking available to accommodate family/caregivers, visitors, and staff. It is also recommended that a minimum of two (2) parking spaces be identified as parking for those with a disability and that these spaces be at least 13 feet wide and located near the entrance door.

When necessary, arrangements should be made with local authorities to provide safety zones for those arriving by motor vehicle and adequate traffic signals for people entering and exiting the facility.

140	Outside space that is used for outdoor activities shall be safe, accessible to indoor areas, and accessible to those with a disability.

Guideline:
This area could include smooth walkways, seating for resting or watching activities, recreational space, and a garden area. The area should have a fence or landscaping to create a boundary in order to prevent participants from wandering away, and it should be easily supervised by staff. Outside furniture should be sturdy and safely arranged.

ATMOSPHERE AND DESIGN

Background
The physical environment and design features support the functioning of all participants, accommodate behaviors, and maximize functional abilities, promote safety, and encourage independence and dignity of participants.

The atmosphere must be warm and inviting. It is desirable to avoid an institutional appearance and to offer an atmosphere that affords an opportunity for social contacts, both casual and structured, but also allows for individuals who prefer being alone from time to time.

It is necessary to create an environment that provides appropriate levels of light, noise, odor, and color conducive to the comfort of older persons. The careful choice of colors and textures will reduce excess sensory stimulation, provide cues and direction, and enhance differentiation of surfaces.

141	The design shall facilitate the participants' movement throughout the center and encourage involvement in activities and services.

Guidelines:
The environment reinforces orientation and awareness of the surroundings by providing cues and information about specific rooms, locations, and functions that help the participant orient to time and space. Interior signs can be used to facilitate participants' ability to move about the center independently and safely.

It is recommended that these cues include the extensive use of signs and the color coding of specific areas of the facility.

---

142 Illumination in all areas shall be adequate and glare shall be avoided.

Guideline:
Attention should be paid to lighting in transitional areas, such as doorways from outside to inside and hallways between different areas of the center.

---

143 Sound transmission shall be controlled.

Guidelines:
Excessive noise, such as fan noise, should be avoided.

Recommended methods of sound control may include acoustical ceiling surfaces, sound deadening carpeting, fabric hangings, partitions between activity areas, and separation of noisy rooms (such as the kitchen) from other areas of the center.

Amplification devices such as assistive listening devices, public address (PA) systems, and audio loops for those with hearing impairment are recommended for consideration.

---

144 Conditions shall be maintained within a comfortable temperature range to accommodate the population served.

Guideline:
Excessive drafts should be avoided uniformly throughout the center.

---

145 Sufficient furnishings shall be available for the entire participant population present.

Guidelines:

Furnishings should accommodate the needs of participants and be attractive, comfortable, and homelike, while being sturdy and safe.

Considerations for selecting furniture may include washability, safety, and the use of arrangements that encourage independence and, perhaps, small group interaction. Recliners can be used as therapeutic tools for rest and/or enhancing circulation and breathing.

According to the needs of participants and the range of services provided (for example, for skin or wound care), beds, cots, or recliners should be available in a designated area.

146	An adult day service facility shall be visible, and the entrance to the center shall be clearly identified.

Guidelines:

Outside signs can be useful to attract participants and to educate the community. It is recommended that signs be visible from the road, appropriate for a service for adults, and printed in large lettering.

Directional signs may also be needed if the entrance to the center is not at the front of the building.

The entrance to the facility should be appealing and protective for participants and others.

The entrance should be well lighted, accessible to individuals with a disability, and located a short distance from the point of arrival.

Also recommended is a covering over the outside entrance to protect participants from inclement weather. The ideal entrance would have a canopy under which drivers could drop off and pick up participants.

147	A telephone shall be available for participant use.

SAFETY AND SANITATION

148	The facility and grounds shall be safe, clean, and accessible to all participants.

149 The facility shall be designed, constructed, and maintained in compliance with all applicable local, state, and federal health and safety regulations.

150 For programs that store medications, there shall be an area for labeled medications, secured and stored apart from participant activity areas.

Guideline:
If medications need to be refrigerated, they should be in a locked box—if not in a separate refrigerator.

151 Safe and sanitary handling, storing, preparation, and serving of food shall be assured.

Guideline:
If meals are prepared on the premises, kitchen appliances, procedures, and equipment must meet state and local requirements.

152 Toxic substances, whether for activities or cleaning, shall be stored in a locked area not accessible to participants.

153 At least two well-identified exits shall be available.

154 Signalling devices shall be installed or placed in the rest areas, restroom stalls, and showers.

Intent:
Alarm/warning systems are necessary to ensure the safety of the participants in the center and to alert staff to potentially dangerous situations.

155 The center shall provide a secure environment.

Guideline:
It is recommended that an alarm system be used for participants who wander. It is also recommended that an alarm/warning system be installed at exit ways not regularly used by participants.

156 Universal Precautions shall be used by all staff.

Guideline:
This means that all participants should be considered infected. Staff, including volunteers, should consistently use Universal Body Substance Precautions that presume that any participant may harbor infectious agents in moist secretions and blood. Precautions dictate that protective measures, such as proper handwashing and the proper use of gloves, gowns, and goggles, be used consistently with all participants.

157 An evacuation plan shall be posted in each room.

158 The facility shall be free of hazards.

Guidelines:

Hazards include, for example, high steps, steep grades, and exposed electrical cords.

Steps and curbs should be painted and the edges of stairs marked appropriately to highlight them.

Nonslip surfaces or bacteria-resistant carpets should be provided on stairs, ramps, and interior floors.

159 All stairs, ramps, and bathrooms accessible to those with a disability shall be equipped with properly anchored handrails.

160 If the functional level of any of the participants requires such assistance, then handrails shall be installed throughout the center.

161 Procedures for fire safety as approved by the state or local fire authority shall be adopted and posted.

Guidelines:

Included are provisions for fire drills, inspection and maintenance of fire extinguishers, periodic inspection, and training by fire department personnel. The center should conduct and document quarterly fire drills and keep reports of drills on file. Improvements should be made based on the fire drill evaluation. Smoke detectors should also be used.

Sprinkler systems and carbon monoxide detectors are also recommended.

162 Emergency first aid kits shall be visible and accessible to staff.

Guideline:
Contents of the kits should be replenished after use and inventoried regularly. Personnel trained in first aid and CPR should be on hand whenever participants are present.

163 There shall be sufficient maintenance and housekeeping personnel to assure that the facility is clean, sanitary, and safe at all times.

Guideline:
Maintenance and housekeeping should be carried out on a regular schedule and in conformity with generally accepted sanitation standards, without interfering with the program.

164 Insect infestation control shall be scheduled at a time when participants are not in the center.

165 Equipment shall be adequately and safely maintained. A sufficient budget shall be provided for equipment maintenance, repair, or replacement.

166 Smoking shall be permitted only in an adequately ventilated and supervised special area away from the main program area.

Special guidelines when serving individuals with cognitive impairment:
The physical facility and operation should both protect the participant from injury and maintain his or her rights at the same time. In addition to the requirements of the overall standards, the facility should:

- offer greater square footage of common activity space per participant than the overall standards require (preferably 80 - 100 square feet per participant);
- be self-contained, if possible, with a minimal number of passageways, corridors, and exit doors;
- provide reduced sensory stimulation;
- make careful use of safety precautions;
- be free of ambiguities and obstacles;
- use locks in accordance with local fire and safety requirements;
- use no physical restraints, unless ordered by a physician;
- use modifications, such as disguised doors (in accordance with local fire and safety requirements) to control wandering;
- test out modifications to the environment prior to full implementation;
- offer a space for personal belongings (including a change of clothing);
- provide at least one toilet for every six (6) participants;
- provide a shower area for participants who are incontinent;
- make special arrangements for fire drills with a plan that decreases stress and anxiety;
- store all materials in a secure place that is inaccessible to participants and use non-toxic materials when possible; and
- minimize multiple sensory stimuli.

PART SEVEN: EVALUATION

BACKGROUND

Evaluations provide information concerning effectiveness in reaching established goals and objectives. Evaluation is an ongoing, continuous process whereby information is secured by the center to make appropriate program and/or structural changes. Evaluations include an analysis of data collected and a comparison of the planned expectations and actual achievements, based on prevailing community standards of care and benchmarks for adult day service care.

Program evaluation may be conducted either internally or externally. If conducted internally, evaluators should also include individuals not directly affiliated with the center. If conducted externally, the interdisciplinary team should include persons with expertise about the population being served in the center.

The National Adult Day Services Association is developing an accreditation process, in collaboration with a national accrediting body. When such accreditation is in place, compliance with it will be the most relevant means of identifying and assuring quality. In the meantime, other measures continue to be appropriate.

---

167 Each adult day services program shall have and implement a quality assurance or quality improvement plan for the evaluation of its operation and services.

Guidelines:
The program's goals and objectives should be reviewed at least annually, but not all evaluation components may need to be done that often. The plan should include:
- the purpose and reason for the evaluation;
- the timetable for initiating and completing the evaluation;
- the parties to be involved;
- the areas that will be addressed;
- the methods to be used in conducting the evaluation;
- how the information will be used once it is completed;
- with whom the information will be shared;
- outcomes;
- data gathering; and
- analysis of results and impact.

Funding to cover the costs of program evaluation should be included in the program budget.

---

168 The ongoing evaluation process shall examine the adult day services program on three levels: the participant/caregiver/staff level, the center/program level, and the community level.

Guidelines:

The evaluation should include resources invested, the productivity of performance, and the resulting benefits, as measured by outcomes and levels of satisfaction.

Program evaluation is done regularly, and results are reported to the governing body. The governing body must ensure that evaluations result in positive and constructive actions for improving center effectiveness (See also "Part Two:Administration and Organization," page 21).

There should be a quality assurance component that routinely and continuously assesses and measures the impact of the program on the participants, family/caregivers, and the community to determine that the program is meeting their needs. This component may include:
- participant and/or family/caregiver satisfaction with service and evaluation as part of an exit survey;
- data collected from the grievance procedure;
- community surveys;
- ongoing care plan review and evaluation and random review of records by the interdisciplinary team;
- an objective participant assessment tool that measures social, health, functional, and cognitive status at intake and at regular intervals thereafter;
- utilization review, and
- development and implementation of quality improvement projects.

These tools can be used to measure both individual and group outcomes, to identify the program's strengths and weaknesses, and to provide some guidance for program improvement.

---

169 Each center shall develop policies and procedures for monitoring continuous quality improvement and determining further action.

Guidelines:
The policies and procedures should be developed by the administrator with the advice of the interdisciplinary staff team and the advisory committee (Standard 8, page 22) and with the approval of the governing body.

The quality assurance plan should include provision for a utilization review committee, a care plan audit (completed by a staff member, as determined by the center), an infection control committee, periodic record audits, and a measure of participant and/or family/caregiver satisfaction. Participant outcomes should be measured and the cost-effectiveness of the program should be assessed.

The utilization review committee, if composed of persons not employed by the center, will benefit from similar professional training to, and communication with, center staff. Duties of the utilization review committee are:
- to evaluate appropriateness of admissions;
- to evaluate adequacy and coordination of provided services;
- to evaluate continued stay, length of stay, and discharge practices; and
- to recommend in writing corrective action to the administrator.

If a utilization review is conducted by a funding source, those results may be substituted for a review by a utilization review committee.

Care plan audits, evaluating quality of care in relation to criteria established by the interdisciplinary team, should follow these essential steps:
- development of outcome criteria, for presenting problems common to the center's participants;
- data on actual outcomes, as abstracted from the center's records;
- evaluation of actual outcomes compared with the outcome criteria, to identify problem areas;
- documented submission of recommended corrective action to the program director; and
- reassessment of the appropriateness of the recommended corrective action, as revealed by the improved outcomes of the next audit.

An infection control committee has responsibility for monitoring procedures implemented to guard against the spread of communicable disease and basic hygienic policies and procedures.

Periodic record audits will determine accuracy and timeliness of all data recorded.

A measure of participant/family/caregiver satisfaction, such as periodic satisfaction questionnaires, discharge interviews, or informal discussion groups, is an important indicator of the responsiveness of the center to participant and family/caregiver needs. It will highlight areas of excellence and areas that need improvement (Also see 168, page 91).

Measures - Guidelines for quality improvement:

The following measures of quality are recommended for specific aspects of the center's operations.

Fiscal—The fiscal system and fiscal plan should be evaluated in comparison to the standards in this document and to those of the center's governing body.

Facility—The facility should be evaluated in comparison to the standards in this document and a plan developed to address needs regarding location and space, atmosphere and design, safety and sanitation, and comfort.

Records and Data—Each organization should establish a record-keeping system that meets the external state licensing/certification/funding requirements, and the ongoing internal management needs of the organization; meets internal program goals for client services; and supports service delivery. Each record-keeping system should be evaluated according to the standards in this document and to those of the governing body.

Services—Services provided should be evaluated in comparison to the standards in this document, with particular emphasis on the level and intensity of services in relation to participant needs.

Personnel—Personnel policies and records should be evaluated according to the standards in this document and to those of the governing body.

Marketing—Objectives and the tools and techniques used in marketing should be evaluated as a component part of strategic planning. Marketing should be evaluated in relation to community image (including potential referral sources and consumer groups), the census of the program (the number of people served and the target population), and the number of appropriate versus inappropriate referrals.

Administration—The authority structure, including board of directors, administration, and federal/state/local government, should be evaluated in terms of its relationship to the goals of the organization.

It is recommended that the administrative areas evaluated include:
- a mission statement that directs policy;
- organizational structure;
- decision-making authority; and
- relationship of governing body to operations and the advisory committee.

170	An overall plan for and commitment to quality shall be considered by each adult day services program.

Guideline:

For example, the center may consider a system such as total quality management, a process guided by the principles that businesses should be customer-focused, dedicated to continually improving services in measurable ways, and committed to creating a work environment that supports those goals. A key element is data collection that makes it possible to measure performance and track progress, resulting in the process of continuous quality improvement.

GLOSSARY

accreditation - the process by which an agency or organization evaluates and recognizes a program or institution as meeting certain predetermined standards; not applied to individuals

activities of daily living (ADLs) - functions or tasks for self-care usually performed in the normal course of a day, including mobility, bathing, dressing, toileting, transferring, and eating

acuity - measurement of an individual's degree of impairment indicating the amount of care needed; the higher the acuity, the more intense the service

adult day services - community-based group programs designed to meet the needs of adults with impairments through individual plans of care; structured, comprehensive, non-residential programs that provide health, social, and related support services in a protective setting

ancillary - extra or additional

assessment - a comprehensive written description which evaluates the participant's strengths, weaknesses, problems, and needs, and also addresses how the center will serve the participant

audioloop - system of amplifying or magnifying sound within a defined area, linking into individual hearing aids

care management - a component of the community care system: a process of management which includes assessing the individual's functional level and impairments, developing a plan of care, identifying and arranging for coordinated delivery of services, monitoring charges, and periodically reassessing needs

certification - a mechanism by which a nongovernmental agency or association grants recognition to an individual who has met certain predetermined qualifications specified by that agency

cognitive impairment - a weakening or deterioration of the mental processes of perception, memory, judgement, and reasoning

community-based - in the groups, agencies, or programs in a given geographic area, not within a residential institution

core services - basic, fundamental services essential to all adult day service programs

counseling - an interactive process, on a one-to-one or group basis, in which an individual is provided guidance and assistance in the utilization of services and help in coping with personal problems through the establishment of a supportive relationship

enhanced services - augmented, larger or greater, services, in addition to core services

functional impairment - the limitation of an individual's functional ability, the inability to perform personal and instrumental activities of daily living and associated tasks, or the inability to establish and maintain an independent living arrangement

functional maintenance - a level of therapy services designed to maintain maximum functional capacity and avoid deterioration to the point of requiring the repetition of skilled interventions

holistic - treating the person as a whole—with recognition of his or her mental, physical, emotional, social, and spiritual aspects—while acknowledging his or her relationship to the broader systems of family and community

individual plan of care - a written plan of services designed to provide the participant with appropriate services and treatment in accordance with his or her assessed needs

in-kind contribution - payment made or given in goods, commodities, space, services, or time rather than money

instrumental activities of daily living (IADLs) - functions or tasks of independent living, including shopping, housework, meal preparation and cleanup, laundry, taking medication, money management, transportation, correspondence, telephoning, and related tasks

intensive services - specialized, skilled care provided by trained, licensed professional staff

interdisciplinary team (or multi-disciplinary team) - all staff members responsible for the care of each participant who, together, assess the participant, make recommendations on interventions and services to be offered, and provide direct services

levels of care - distinctions based upon the scope and intensity of supervision, assistance, treatment, and service provided

long-term care - a coordinated continuum of preventive, diagnostic, therapeutic, rehabilitative, supportive, and maintenance services that address the health, social, and personal needs of individuals who have restricted self-care capabilities

NICLC - the National Institute on Community-based Long-term Care, a constituent unit of The National Council on the Aging, Inc.

paraprofessional - a person trained to assist a professional but not licensed to practice in the profession

personal care - care provided to assist an individual with his/her ADLs

physician, staff - a physician employed by the adult day services center

policies - guidelines, rules, and directives within which employees must perform their work, as established by the governing body of an organization

procedures - detailed methods by which policies are implemented

psychosocial - involving both psychological and social aspects

quality assurance - any evaluation of services provided and result achieved that is made in comparison to accepted standards

respite - short-term, intermittent, substitute care provided for a person with impairments in the absence of the regular caregiver

restorative or rehabilitative services - services intended to restore the individual to his/her optimal level of functioning

risk management - assessment and control of obvious and identifiable risks to which a program might be subject; involves analyzing all possibilities of loss and determining how to reduce exposure

strategic plan - plan, method, or series for obtaining specific goals or results, usually on a multi-year basis

therapeutic - describes services and/or activities intended to be beneficial and related to treatment or to the plan of care

therapeutic milieu - a total environment in which all that occurs is directed toward improving the quality of life of the participant with services and/or activities intended to be beneficial and related to treatment or to the plan of care

unit dose - a pre-measured amount of medication

Universal Precautions - infection control guidelines developed by the Centers for Disease Control, intended to protect the worker against transmission of infectious diseases through exposure to blood and certain other body fluids

INDEX